2. BOLUP (OCT. 2003)

2

Sorting Out the Web

Recent Titles in
Contemporary Studies in Information Management, Policies, and
Services
Peter Hernon, Series Editor

Sorting Out the Web

Approaches to Subject Access

Candy Schwartz

CONTEMPORARY STUDIES IN INFORMATION
MANAGEMENT, POLICIES, AND SERVICES
Peter Hernon, Series Editor

ABLEX PUBLISHING
Westport, Connecticut • London

Library of Congress Cataloging-in-Publication Data

Schwartz, Candy.
  Sorting out the web : approaches to subject access / by Candy Schwartz.
      p.   cm.—(Contemporary studies in information management, policies,
  and services)
    Includes bibliographical references and index.
    ISBN 1–56750–518–X—ISBN 1–56750–519–8 (pbk.)
    1. World Wide Web—Subject access.   2. Web search engines.   I. Title.
  II. Series.
  ZA4232.S39   2001
  025.04—dc21   00–022370

British Library Cataloguing in Publication Data is available.

Library of Congress Catalog Card Number: 00–022370
ISBN: 1–56750–518–X
       1–56750–519–8 (pbk.)

First published in 2001

Ablex Publishing, 88 Post Road West, Westport, CT 06881
An imprint of Greenwood Publishing Group, Inc.
www.ablexbooks.com

Printed in the United States of America

The paper used in this book complies with the
Permanent Paper Standard issued by the National
Information Standards Organization (Z39.48–1984).

10 9 8 7 6 5 4 3 2 1

04652671

Contents

Figures

Preface

I have always been fascinated with classification and order. As a two-year-old in the wilds of northern Canada, where "proper" toys were hard to come by, I could be happily diverted with a tin of nails or a box of buttons to sort—by size, shape, color, whatever. A few years later, back in the city, I created vast paper doll worlds of families with sets of children who were perfectly matched by age and gender, and, oddly enough, I deliberately chose for them names with many natural language variations (e.g., Elizabeth, because it could be Beth, Eliza, Liz, Liza, Libby, and so on). And, of course, in my adult life, my record collection, spice racks, bookshelves, and closets are the epitome of organization (although chaos is always allowed a little bit of space—the "miscellaneous" drawer).

Small wonder that I chose the study of language for my undergraduate degree, librarianship as a graduate program, cataloging as my first professional career, and automatic classification as a dissertation topic, and that I ended up teaching in areas related to classification, indexing, and database management. It is also no surprise that I am captivated by the Web—chaos in need of organization. Over the past decade I have been keeping track of efforts to impose that organization, from the World Wide Web Virtual Library to search engines and subject gateways. This book is my attempt to look systematically at those efforts, to explore the tools used for subject access, and to share some thoughts about what they have to offer now and in the future.

There is an inherent problem in trying to capture in print anything related to the Web. Even within the space of the two years over which I put these chapters together, the application of classification and indexing to networked resources has changed dramatically. Writing about these systems becomes a matter of having to say, at some point, "stop here," knowing full well that the Internet, like rust, never sleeps. However, while the implementations may be altered, the concepts presented in these chapters are fundamental, and the foundations of subject access have proven solid enough to withstand and adapt to change. I also faced another problem in trying to describe organizing systems which merit far more space than I could allow, and having to omit, or give very short shrift to, areas of study worthy of far deeper treatment. Nonetheless, it is my hope that this book will be of value to people already interested in indexing and classification, as well as those who are developing subject access systems, whether in libraries or in other settings.

I would like to dedicate this work to my editor, Peter Hernon, whose gentle nudging kept me on track; to F.W. Lancaster and the late Gerard Salton, whose publications opened my eyes to a different world during my master's degree work; to my husband, whose uncomplaining patience and support during periods of frenetic work is much appreciated; and most of all, to my best friend and mother, Mary Brown, who passed away shortly after this manuscript was submitted, and who knew never to ask how the book was coming along.

1

Introduction

[The World Wide Web] has evolved into what might be thought of as a chaotic repository for the collective output of the world's digital "printing presses." This storehouse of information contains not only books and papers, but raw scientific data, menus, meeting minutes, advertisements, video and audio recordings, and transcripts of interactive conversations. The ephemeral mixes everywhere with works of lasting importance. (Lynch, 1997, p. 52)

Some have characterized the Internet as a library with no collection development policy, where all the books have been dumped on the floor in no particular order. Others have likened Internet searching to "drinking from a firehose." In the autonomous, idiosyncratic, and some would say anarchic, world of networked information, this situation is slow to change. In fact, there is a certain charm in the disorder. However, libraries with no catalogs, encyclopedias with no indexes, or disciplines with no indexing services would not be considered charming for very long. It is not surprising that the introduction of every protocol for information transfer on the Internet has been followed by the development of tools intended to promote subject search through resources available under that protocol—for example, archie for file transfer protocol (FTP), veronica for Gopher, and search engines for the World Wide Web (WWW).

Comparing the Internet to a library is appropriate, as the former is a collection of information resources, as is the latter. We speak of the "virtual library" as something different from an ordinary library, as if the knowledge contained in traditional libraries is bounded by the walls of a building. This is not true, as libraries have provided access to information resources not contained in their collections for centuries. The principal difference has more to do with the values added by library processes—selection, description, organization, and location assistance. This book will explore those processes for their contribution to resolving the problems of information retrieval in the networked world.

HISTORICAL OVERVIEW

Information Services

People who are in the business of gathering information resources and providing information services have been dealing with issues of knowledge representation and information retrieval since the days of clay tablets and papyrus rolls. Throughout most of history and using the technology at hand (see Figure 1.1), the knowledge forming the intellectual storehouses managed by information specialists (be they temple priests, librarians and archivists, or information systems managers) has had a more or less physical being. That is, it has been contained in some relatively fixed physical format, such as a book, a journal article, a human expert, a film, an artifact (e.g., a laboratory specimen), or a machine-readable data file residing in some specific storage location. Furthermore, most of the collections of these information resources have been constrained in size—defined by boundaries of ownership, location, subject, or some other criterion ("the holdings of the College Library," "the journal literature in the field of education," or "employees of ABC, Inc."). The first step in looking for a specific piece of information has there-

Figure 1.1

Tools of the Trade

<table>
<tr><td colspan="2" align="center">**OVER THE MILLENNIA**</td></tr>
<tr><td align="center">**Information-Recording Tools**</td><td align="center">**Information-Carrying Devices**</td></tr>
<tr><td align="center">charred wood</td><td align="center">stone, pebbles</td></tr>
<tr><td align="center">sharpened sticks</td><td align="center">bone, wood</td></tr>
<tr><td align="center">sharpened stones</td><td align="center">string</td></tr>
<tr><td align="center">styli, reeds</td><td align="center">wax, clay</td></tr>
<tr><td align="center">beads</td><td align="center">metal</td></tr>
<tr><td align="center">knots</td><td align="center">hide</td></tr>
<tr><td align="center">brushes</td><td align="center">bark</td></tr>
<tr><td align="center">feathers, quills</td><td align="center">parchment, papyrus</td></tr>
<tr><td align="center">pens</td><td align="center">cloth, paper</td></tr>
<tr><td align="center">metal type</td><td align="center">plastic</td></tr>
<tr><td align="center">electrostatic powder</td><td align="center">film</td></tr>
<tr><td align="center">electromagnetic impulses</td><td align="center">magnetic storage devices</td></tr>
<tr><td align="center">laser beams</td><td align="center">optical storage devices</td></tr>
</table>

fore typically been to identify the collection or collections which are worth more detailed exploration for their contents.

Most of the systems developed to provide access to these knowledge-bearing formats have been pointing systems—each item in the collection is represented by a surrogate, with sufficient location information to find the actual item once the surrogate has been evaluated. The efficacy of such systems resides in their success in achieving a match between what the user is seeking and what the system has to offer. Various methods of representation and retrieval have evolved over the centuries, changing and adapting as we come to understand more about how people look for information, and as new tools become available (from the papyrus roll to the microcomputer).

Developments in Information Technology

In the latter half of the twentieth century, some of the basic characteristics of information availability changed. Initially these changes were convenient and manageable. A search which used to require laborious browsing through many volumes of a printed indexing and abstracting service could be conducted online through (usually fee-based) dialup database services, or on CD-ROM. More recently, rather than providing a list of bibliographic citations (requiring of the recipient further hunting, duplication, inter-library lending, or ordering), information services make the full text of information sources available in the same databases which used to contain only surrogates, or they provide on-demand full-text sources via mail, fax, or e-mail.

These developments were welcomed by library and information services communities, with generally appropriate adjustments in the tools and methods of access provision (more dramatic adjustments were required in administration, especially in pricing structures and fiscal resource allocation). Similarly, the appearance of online public access catalogs (OPACs) on local area networks (LANs), while requiring a shift in the technological expertise required of today's librarians, did not have a very great impact on the nature of library collections nor on the way items were described in those collections.

The End User

One change that did foreshadow what was to come was a shift in the distribution of the population of information seekers who interacted directly with retrieval systems. Until recently, most computer-based information systems (with the exception of OPACs) were used by library or information staff on behalf of users. This was the result of several factors—online dialup services usually charged by the minute, the search tools and commands used in effective and cost-efficient retrieval were complex and arcane, and the equipment was expensive and not widely available. During the 1980s, and continuing into the 1990s, decreasing computing costs and increasing processing speed and storage capacities made the telecommunicating computer an ubiquitous component of the business and academic workplace and the home, at least for certain segments of the population at large. Concomitant advances were made in the study of human–computer interaction, and in the design of software and hardware to facilitate it. In other words, a significant percentage of the information-using public became potentially capable of using information retrieval systems directly, without intermediation.

That market was recognized by commercial information service providers, which were possibly also influenced by the thought that traditional library markets, never very wealthy to begin with, might reach saturation. CompuServe and The Source were two of the first dialup information services directed specifically to end users—many more were to follow. Services of this type typically provided a mix of their own proprietary content and pass-through access to other content providers (most notably Dialog). At the same time, companies with traditional library markets began to develop alternative interfaces and pricing structures for direct use by end users (e.g., Dialog's Knowledge Index). Some of these services were targeted to specific niche markets (frequently the legal and medical professions, for obvious reasons), some were format-specific (for instance, customized news services incorporating newspapers, wire services, and industry newsletters), and some were designed to appeal to the family, offering a smattering of popular information, reference sources, useful software, games, bulletin boards, and the like.

These developments caused some mild concern in the library community, especially in the light of advertising copy in the nonlibrary professional press, with slogans such as "be your own librarian" or "you don't need to go into the library anymore." Still, the general feeling seemed to be that mediated use of information systems would still be necessary for in-depth research, as end-user search software did not supply sufficiently sophisticated capabilities for cost-effective retrieval. Also, library and information specialists were more familiar with, and had access to, a wider range of machine-readable resource collections than would be provided by one, or even several, content providers. Individuals were unlikely to maintain contracts with multiple providers, or to subscribe to costly CD-ROM databases.

The Internet

The Internet arrived. In its infancy, in the 1960s, use was generally restricted to the research community. Gradually this expanded to include the academic community at large and the business world. Initially networking was used for e-mail, file sharing, electronic conferencing, and bulletin boards. In the mid-1980s gopher was introduced, along with Wide Area Information Server (WAIS) at around the same time, and the World Wide Web by the beginning of the 1990s. In all three, there was a focus on organizing and retrieving information based on its subject content. Advances in networking hardware and software in general brought the Internet to any machine with dialup capabilities, and the network went "graphic," making it easier to use and consistent with the customary Windows and Macintosh platforms on desktops. The same time period saw the startup of a plethora of independent Internet service providers (ISPs), opening up access to any person or company willing to pay a nominal monthly fee. Suddenly hundreds of thousands (and eventually millions) of individuals and commercial concerns were able to use the Internet, and, perhaps more significantly, to make information available on it.

THE LIBRARY RESPONSE

As with other technological advances, libraries have adapted to this innovation. Working with local information systems staff, librarians have started hundreds of discussion groups and bulletin boards (see Library-Oriented Lists and Electronic Serials, http:// www.wrlc.org/liblists/), mounted library gophers and then Web sites, provided Internet access and training for their user communities, and incorporated networked resources and Web search engines into their personal toolkits. By the end of the twentieth century, almost all North American and many European libraries have established a presence on the Web, including, in many cases, graphical browser access to their OPACs. The library community has become involved in the development of interoperability standards such as the Z39.50 *Information Retrieval Service Definition & Protocol Specifications for Library Applications*. Most recently, libraries have begun to apply subject analysis tools and methods developed for library systems to the systematic organization of Internet resources, and have become involved in large-scale metadata and digital library projects.

Who better to help "untangle the Web" than a community which has been concerned with organization and access since the beginnings of librarianship? Although no one expects that there will be a serious attempt to "catalog" the entire Internet, successful projects in improving access to networked resources are likely to arise from the collaborative efforts of librarians, information retrieval specialists, computer scientists, linguists, and experts from other disciplines. To become partners in such ventures, new library and information professionals will need to be familiar with different types of access tools and strategies, and will need to be able to make decisions about what is appropriate for different resources, settings, and communities.

This book looks at efforts to provide methods and tools which support subject retrieval of networked information resources. It is directed at practicing librarians and information professionals, students of library and information science (LIS), and those who wish to find out more about subject approaches to networked information resource discovery. Chapter 2 introduces the concept of metadata, which is really more about potentiating subject description (and other characteristics of networked resources) than about actual description. Chapters 3 and 4 deal with the use of intellectually created devices—classification and alphabetical subject languages. Chapter 5 is concerned with Web search engines, and takes an in-depth look at the variations among these largely automatic tools. Chapter 6 considers trends in subject description and access—what is around the corner, or in the information retrieval laboratory?

Rather than pepper the text or the list of references with any more URLs than necessary, the reader is referred at the end of most chapters to one or more Web pages on subject access. These pages provide annotated links to the various projects, products, and sites mentioned in the text, and to many of the Web-based resources listed in reference lists. These pages will be kept up to date for the (working) life of the author, as they are the result of a personal and abiding desire to keep up to date in areas of intense interest and rapid change.

REFERENCE

Lynch, Clifford. (1997). Searching the Internet. *Scientific American*, 276(3), 52–56.

2

Metadata

In the mid-1990s the term "metadata," thus far used primarily in the field of database management and information systems design, began to emerge in the LIS literature on resource description, and also captured the interest of scholarly and commercial content providers and the Internet standards-making community. Within a few years, metadata had become a common topic in print and electronic communications in both these fields, and even appeared in the pages of *Scientific American* (Bosak & Bray, 1999). In fact, the concept is far from foreign to LIS, since many of the activities related to the provision of metadata are forms of cataloging and representation, which librarians have been involved with since the beginnings of librarianship.

BACKGROUND

The pat answer to the question "What are (or is) metadata?" is "Metadata are data about data." The term metadata is used (rather loosely) to characterize data which describe or in some way complement or supplement a networked resource, additionally to what that resource may say about itself. For example, library staff might choose to catalog certain Web sites for entry into an OPAC. These catalog records contain metadata about the sites (authors, titles, subject headings, publication information, location, and so on).

Many different types of metadata might be associated with a networked resource, each serving a different purpose:

Descriptive

- Content description (including subject access); and
- Content rating and evaluation.

Administrative

- Terms and conditions of use;
- Provenance (e.g., original source, date, and agency of creation);
- Processing information (e.g., file format, processing history); and
- Linkage (e.g., relationships between objects).

Structural

- Information about necessary enabling elements (e.g., to enable page-turning in an electronic text).

Domain-specific metadata (e.g., for cultural heritage resources or government information access) may add yet more types (e.g., see Baca, 1998). Some metadata can be generated automatically from examination of the object, while some is created intellectually.

Selected Literature

The notion of "cataloging the Internet" (or at least a portion of it) had taken hold by the mid-1990s, and Caplan's (1995) report on the OCLC/NCSA Metadata Workshop and the birth of the Dublin Core (discussed later in this chapter) was one of the first to bring the concept of "metadata" to a broad spectrum of the LIS community. In a few brief paragraphs, she manages to capture the spirit of the meeting and to make the case for continuing the effort. Weibel's (1995) summary of the same event for a different audience (digital library researchers) is more technical and of greater depth, but largely has the same effect. From that point forward, hardly an LIS conference went by without one or more sessions on metadata. Heery (1996) and Vellucci (1996) offer extended surveys of different metadata options, and, although what was known at the time about the specific schemes may be a bit dated, in each case the general discussion and insight is still valid and valuable. Dempsey and Heery (1998) take a detailed look at definitions and examples, leading to a typology of approaches, while, on the other end of the spectrum, Hudgins, Agnew, and Brown's (1999) practical introduction and survey of almost 20 different resource description practices considers the "potential for libraries" for each, and also includes a set of guidelines for project implementation. Milstead and Feldman (1999a, 1999b) review various approaches and look at metadata from the point of view of its impact on search engines and trained searcher behavior. Lange and Winkler (1997) and Vellucci (1999) provide recent state-of-the-art reviews, each of which is an excellent general starting point from which to explore specific aspects or types of metadata in depth. Finally, Burnett, Ng, and Park (1999) compare metadata development and metadata standards in the bibliographic and data management communities, on the grounds that "an integrated concept of metadata which emphasizes both the intrinsic and extrinsic dimension of metadata can help us to better understand the interaction of the two approaches in the development of metadata schemes" (p. 1216).

CONTENTS AND CONTAINERS

Discussions of metadata usually concern one or more of three parts: content, container, and delivery. The content is the actual information which describes (or is associated with) the networked object in some way and includes a concern with how it is formulated (e.g., titles are formatted according to the *Anglo-American Cataloguing Rules*). This piece is absent from most metadata standards—a provision may be made for "creator," but no provision may be made for how that name should be formatted and to what authority control rules it is subject. This is appropriate given that a metadata standard may be intended for use by a diverse community with different access and control needs. The container provides a set of elements (for example, author, title, and so on) and a syntax for differentiating among these bits of content—for example, this string of characters is a title, but that string is a publisher—and may include a means for identifying formatting method and possibly more complex structural information. Delivery refers to the means through which metadata are associated with the object to which they pertain. Simple META tags in an HTML (HyperText Markup Language) document (see Figure 2.1) can deliver metadata information, although in many cases metadata are stored separately from the resources which they describe and delivery is more complex.

Each of these components plays a role in metadata provision, and each component is associated with various standards and codes of practices. Other chapters in this book focus on subject content—the alphabetic and systematic subject tools which have been used to enhance access to networked resources. This chapter focuses on element sets, syntax, and delivery.

THE ROLE OF METADATA

Discovery and Retrieval

In the context of the topic of this book, the most interesting role of metadata is to support networked discovery and retrieval, and the most dramatic example of the consequence of an absence of metadata is the Web. The Web being the size that it is (whatever measurement is used), it is very difficult to discriminate among resources "out there" on a given subject, or even to determine where the best starting point is to reach that part of "out there" which might be worth exploring. Resource discovery tools such as search engines and directories, discussed in Chapter 5, offer some limited assistance. However, the larger the size of search service databases, and

Figure 2.1

Simple Metadata in an HTML Document

```
<!DOCTYPE html PUBLIC "-//W3C//DTD XHTML 1.0
transitional//EN" "DTD/xhtml1-transitional.dtd">

<html xmlns="http://www.w3.org/1999/xhtml" xml:lang="en"
lang="en">

<head>

<title>LIS 415, Organization of Knowledge in Libraries, Course
Page</title>

<meta name="author" content="Schwartz, Candy" />
<meta name="keywords" content="Cataloging, Classification"/>

</head>

<body>
.
.
.
[Content displayed by browser]
.
.
.
</body>

</html>
```

the more that financial return overrides concerns about the quality of discovery and retrieval, the less helpful they are likely to become.

Designers of top-level Web pages frequently seek to improve the likelihood of those pages appearing in the first 10 of search engine results. This has given rise to a cottage industry in helping designers create text content intended to influence ranking. These specific instances aside, the text content of networked objects is usually not created with retrieval in mind. Furthermore, many Web pages contain very little text at all, relying largely on images and icons to convey content. Many objects distributed in networked settings are not text files—they may be image, sound, video, or other (including as yet unimagined) formats. Even more dramatically, one might wish to describe a resource which is not networked (a product for sale, for example) or a resource whose content is not publicly available (e.g., an electronic text available only by payment or license). So one important role for metadata is to add descriptive information to objects which do not adequately self-describe or which do not make text available for public searching.

Such descriptive information can serve several different purposes. One obvious function is to support retrieval through the added (and often controlled) terminology found in keywords, subject headings, abstracts or annotations, personal or corporate names, titles, and so on. In addition, if the metadata are contained in a structured format, the structure itself may provide opportunities for fielded search. For example, if a "subject" field forms part of the metadata record, then a search interface might offer the possibility of restricting a query to that field. Currently, in the rare instances where fielded search is available in Web search engines, the fields are extracted from HTML markup, and the only subject-like field made available for fielded search is the title element of the document. By way of comparison, fielded search is the norm in OPACs and commercial online databases, where the underlying record structures are comparatively rich and complex.

Depending on the nature of the metadata, another added value afforded by descriptive representations of networked resources might be to organize search results into something other than a simple list ranked by some measure of likely relevance to the query.

Several Web search engines, the best known example being Northern Light, organize search results into clusters based on a classification scheme to which documents are classified using some automatic algorithm, and/or based on domain (e.g., results from sites whose domain names end in .edu might be grouped into a folder called "Academic"). A collection of resources to which classification numbers have been assigned from a detailed classification scheme (discussed in Chapter 3) offers the possibility of using that scheme to array search results, or using the scheme as one of several entry methods to the collection—that is, to allow browsing through the classification scheme as an alternative to direct search.

Efficiency

Metadata records are usually small representatives of the objects they describe, just as cataloging records are smaller than the items they represent. A collection of metadata information, searchable separately from the objects, presents savings in network bandwidth use and improvements in response time to the user. Also, as Dempsey, Russell, & Heery (1997) remind us, metadata can be addressed to humans, but it also addresses "software tools that will carry out a range of discovery, transaction, use, and other functions on resources."

Furthermore, descriptive information in the metadata record (e.g., title, annotation, subject, size, date, software requirements, and contents evaluation) can be used to enhance review of search results. Users could be offered format choices—a short format for quick browsing (perhaps title only) and one or more richer formats to allow users to choose which resources are worth further exploration. This hearkens back to one of Charles Ammi Cutter's (1904) principles of catalog design—a representation should offer information which allows users to evaluate an item bibliographically (e.g., by publication date, edition, etc.) and for its character (through displaying subject headings, notes, and so on).

Another aspect of efficiency has to do with repetition and redundancy. If metadata regarding the protection of intellectual property, or the need to negotiate for the use of an object, is the same for a set of objects, it makes more sense to store that information once than to repeat it as part of the content of each object.

Finally, institutions adhering to the same metadata standard or to standards which are interoperable can share information, much as institutions adhering to standard library cataloging practices share cataloging records though bibliographic utilities such as OCLC, Inc. They can also engage in cooperative metadata creation efforts. The benefits of such cooperation include avoiding duplication of effort, presenting a common interface across collections maintained by different institutions (or at least common search capabilities), and generally augmenting the size of the collection of resources available to searchers.

Managing Metadata

Figure 2.1 showed descriptive metadata stored within a resource. Alternatively metadata can be stored separately, with links to local or remote resources (similar to the library catalog model). Then again the metadata may be remote, distributed, and even multitype, accessed through a query management system. One advantage to storing metadata records with the resources they describe, or having direct control over the resources themselves, is the greater power this affords for maintaining accuracy in representation. Even within what is supposedly a circumscribed network, and more so on the Internet, networked resources vanish, change location, or change content. Despite the availability of automatic agents which can check links, keeping metadata records up to date is a daunting and time-consuming task. Powell (1997) and Weibel (1997) discuss models and issues in metadata management.

BEFORE WE KNEW IT WAS METADATA

While the term "metadata" only started to be used fairly recently, the concept of providing searchable representations of Internet resources is certainly not new. Forward-looking institutions and information service providers were quick to create Web-accessible databases containing descriptions of networked objects. Such initiatives were not able to make use of existing standards or tools described in the remainder of this chapter. In addition to being the work of early adopters, these projects are typically characterized by being small collections, in constrained subject areas, targeted to specific (but public) user communities, and not intended to be part of larger cooperative record exchange. In some cases, such ventures have migrated to metadata standards as these began to emerge.

Recently the term "subject gateways" has appeared as a way to describe resource directories which make use of metadata and other tools to support discovery and retrieval. In his overview for a special issue of *Online Information Review* on gateways, Koch (2000) makes a distinction between general subject gateways (which could include a simple annotated and categorized list of links) and what he calls "quality-controlled" subject gateways—those which add value through resource selection, collection development and maintenance, rich descriptive metadata, and the application of controlled vocabularies and classification. Many of the examples in this and subsequent chapters are gateways of this latter kind.

The INFOMINE project offers a good example of a pioneer project. INFOMINE was initiated in 1994 by staff at the library of the University of California, Riverside, with the intention of providing Web-based access to substantial research and educational Internet (and other electronic) resources in all major disciplines (Mitchell & Mooney, 1996). The database architecture is based on the SQL (Structured Query Language) standard, and programmers have developed interfaces for simple and sophisticated searching, browsing, and record editing and submission. Subject-related fields in INFOMINE metadata records include title, Library of Congress subject headings (this application is discussed further in Chapter 4), keywords, and an annotation (see Figure 2.2). In addition to receiving a substantial volume of use, INFOMINE has been widely praised and is included in various directories.

CATALOGING THE WEB

No one (I hope) seriously believes that the entire Web can be cataloged using typical library procedures, nor would it even be a

Figure 2.2

An INFOMINE Record

Title:
Find A Hospice: National Hospice and Palliative Care Organization
Database

Related Subjects:
HOSPICES—UNITED STATES—DIRECTORIES

Related Keywords:
DATABASES
DIRECTORIES
SEARCHABLE

Related Title Words:
FIND A HOSPICE: NATIONAL HOSPICE AND PALLIATIVE
CARE ORGANIZATION DATABASE

Related Authors:
NATIONAL HOSPICE AND PALLIATIVE CARE
ORGANIZATION
NHPCO

URL:
http://www.nho.org/database.htm

Annotation:
Your search begins by displaying "a list of countries in the specified
state that are served by hospices. Selecting a country will result in a
list of local Hospices in the surrounding area that serve that county,
complete with contact information." [24230]

Reprinted with permission.

desirable objective given the nature (not to mention the short life span) of much of the content of networked resources. However, there are some advantages to cataloging those sites which are stable, durable, and substantial, and which are judged to be appropriate additions to a library collection under the same criteria used to assess other potential acquisitions. In the current era of browser-accessible OPACs, bibliographic records for remote electronic information become part of the general collection of information which users can search, browse, select from, and retrieve. The tools used to create cataloging records are well understood, widely used by an existing cadre of thousands of trained record creators, and supported and maintained by an administrative infrastructure which includes the Library of Congress and representatives of major national and international library associations. Furthermore, having resource records in MARC (MAchine Readable Cataloging) format means that they are available for cooperative record-sharing.

On the other hand, the traditional tools of cataloging do not accommodate all of the resource description metadata which might be deemed necessary or desirable. This is especially true where establishing relationships among Web objects is concerned. Also, tools designed to describe and control physical objects may not be well suited to their digital counterparts—see, for example, Taylor's (1999) discussion of the problems of applying *Anglo-American Cataloguing Rules* (AACR) to Internet resources. Finally, networked resources fluctuate in location and content (and even existence), and one might wonder whether the time taken to keep track of changes, and to recatalog when necessary, is time well spent.

Many libraries have now incorporated Internet resource cataloging into normal procedures. Changes in the USMARC (now MARC21) format (most notably to accommodate the inclusion of the URL in the 856 field), and helpful manuals such as Olson's (1997) *Cataloging Internet Resources*, mostly derive from Internet cataloging efforts driven by OCLC, Inc.

A Brief Word on MARC

The MARC format has become the foremost container worldwide for library cataloging since its development by the Library of

Congress in the late 1960s. A MARC record consists of three components: the leader (carrying information about the record length, status, type of record, data address, and encoding level), the record directory (providing an index to the location of the fields in the record), and the variable fields (carrying the cataloging information itself). The variable fields include control fields, which hold fixed-length data elements, and the data fields, which include the components of the bibliographic record, as well as some additional descriptive elements. Each field in the MARC record is identified by a field tag, and the data in that field may also be further specified by one or two indicators, which specify some characteristic of the data, and one or more subfield delimiters, which separate field data into smaller units. An example of a MARC record can be seen in Figure 2.3.

Experts have argued for and against the MARC format as a general carrier of Internet resource description, and have called for interaction between MARC and other metadata standards (Barry, 1998; Gaynor, 1996; Guenther, 1994; Hopkins, 1999; Sha, 1995; Vellucci, 1996). On the positive side, the MARC format is a well-established standard with worldwide applications experience, is compact while retaining complexity, and affords flexible display formats. On the other hand, the MARC format takes a linear access approach, making it difficult to cope with hierarchical information or with complex collections requiring connected levels of analysis. Elements needed by some communities are not present in the MARC format or may be present but not isolated within a field for access purposes. Finally, MARC is complex and expensive to apply (in terms of labor) and slow to change (although this could be said of other metadata standards as well).

OCLC Projects

OCLC's first major venture into Web cataloging was the InterCat project, funded by the U.S. Department of Education, Office of Library Programs, from October 1994 through March 1996. With the support of OCLC, staff at volunteer participating institutions created an initial database of cataloged Internet resources and shared

Figure 2.3

A MARC Record

LC Control Number: 99033710

000   01118cam 22002894a 450

001   4049462

005   20000727071022.0

008   990610s1999 flua 000 0 eng

035   __ |9 (DLC) 99033710

906   __ |a 7 |b cbc |c orignew |d 1 |e ocip |f 19 |g y-gencatlg

955   __ |a pc01 to SA00 06-12-99; jb11 06-14-99; jb09 06-15-99; jk14 to DDC 06-15-99; jb00 03-09-00; jb11 06-29-00; jb01 to BCCD 07-27-00

010   __ |a 99033710

020   __ |a 1558747117 (hardcover)

020   __ |a 1558747109 (trade paper)

040   __ |a DLC |c DLC |d DLC

042   __ |a pcc

050   00 |a SF445.5 |b .C47 1999

082   00 |a 636.0188/7 |2 21

245   00 |a Chicken soup for the cat & dog lover's soul : |b celebrating pets as family with stories about *cats, dogs,* and other critters / |c [edited by] Jack Canfield . . . [et al.].

260   __ |a Deerfield Beach, Fla. : |b Health Communications, |c c1999.

300   __ |a xx, 408 p. : |b ill. ; |c 23 cm.

650   _0 |a *Cats* |v Anecdotes.

650   _0 |a *Dogs* |v Anecdotes.

650   _0 |a Pets |v Anecdotes.

650   _0 |a Pet owners |v Anecdotes.

650   _0 |a Human-animal relationships |v Anecdotes.

700   1_ |a Canfield, Jack, |d 1944-

Source: Library of Congress Online Catalog.

their experiences via listserv lists and other electronic forums and conference presentations. The outcomes of this effort were, as mentioned above, modifications to the MARC format, a manual, and a better understanding of the issues and problems. The InterCat database now contains close to 85,000 records but is no longer considered active.

OCLC actively maintains the NetFirst database of Internet resources in the family of FirstSearch reference services. NetFirst metadata displays a hybrid of indexing and abstracting, with Library of Congress subject headings and Dewey Decimal classification numbers.

In January 1999, OCLC embarked on the CORC (Cooperative Online Resource Catalog) project, which extends beyond InterCat in attempting to integrate MARC and established or emerging metadata efforts such as the Dublin Core, Text Encoding Initiative (TEI), Encoded Archival Description (EAD), and eXtensible Markup Language (XML). CORC provides a forum for exploring shared URL maintenance, import and export between various metadata formats, and different methods of presenting CORC information to users (for example, by embedding resource descriptions in pathfinders rather than as individual bibliographic records). Figure 2.4 illustrates the CORC interface.

THE DUBLIN CORE

In March 1995, 52 researchers and practitioners concerned with libraries (traditional and digital) and networking gathered in Dublin, Ohio, to attempt to arrive at a list of descriptive metadata elements intended to promote author-generated resource description which would enhance discovery. There is a precedent for author-generated description in the journal and conference publishing community, where authors are often required to submit indexing and abstracts with articles, but this behavior is driven by a strong incentive (scholarly publication) unrealized in the general Internet publishing communities. Nonetheless, a simple element set, of use to a wide variety of stakeholders, proved in the long run to be well worth the effort. Sponsored by OCLC and a number of other agencies, the

Figure 2.4

The CORC Interface

Search Catalog

for `africa` in `All`

`AND` `folk music` in `Subject`

`AND` [ ] in
- MARC Format
- Name

`AND` [ ] in
- OCLC Number
- Publication Date
- Publication Location
- Publisher
- Standard Number
- Subject
- Title
- URL Phrase
- URL Words

☑ Do relevance ranking.

[Start Search]

Actions: `Displaying Record` 1 ... 6 7 View: `MARC`

OCLC: 44367795 *Entered:* N@F 1998-04-22

Not locked *System:* OCL 2000-06-21

No holdings in GLS and 1 other holding

006		m u
040		N@F ‡c N@F
082	04	338.4762138932
082	04	781.62
082	04	786.919
245	00	Village Pulse Outpost. ‡h [computer file]
260		‡b RootsWorld.
270		‡m hello@rootsworld.com ‡h Feedback
516		World Wide Web Resource
520	8_	Presents Village Pulse Outpost, a record label that specializes in West African drum music, such as Mandinka drum music.

WELCOME TO THE
VILLAGE PULSE OUTPOST

loose consortium of participants has continued to ponder over metadata matters, in annual meetings and in smaller working groups. The second annual meeting resulted in the Warwick Framework, a model suggesting that different packets of metadata can be associated with an object—as opposed to developing one metadata element set which accommodates the needs of all stakeholders and applications.

At the time of this writing, the Dublin Core element set (version 1.1) consists of 15 elements (see Figure 2.5). The Dublin Core community overlaps significantly with standards communities such as the Internet Engineering Task Force (IETF) and the World Wide Web Consortium (W3C). The element set appears as IETF RFC (Request for Comments) 2413 and is promoted in the recent specification issued by the Open eBook Initiative (Open eBook Authoring Group, 1999). The element set has been translated into more than 15 languages, is in use in more than 50 projects, and is employed as a basis for describing official documents in at least two countries (Australia and Denmark).

Tools have been created to aid in use of the Dublin Core, and that use has spread to a wide and diverse community. Embodying the initial project objectives, the Dublin Core is simple (although it accommodates complexity), flexible (and can be adapted to local practices), extensible, and syntax-independent. The elements are optional and repeatable, understandable to many communities, and records can be created using normal editing tools (Figure 2.6 shows an example of embedded Dublin Core in an HTML document). Much of the content can be drawn from intrinsic properties of the object, and some fields (such as format) can be populated algorithmically. Methods for qualifying elements (naming specific authority tools, languages, subfield values, etc.) were released in July 2000.

In addition to CORC (mentioned above), one of the more advanced Dublin Core applications is the Nordic Metadata Project. Funded by NORDINFO, the first phase of the project ran from 1996 to 1998, and was primarily concerned with laying the groundwork for the use of metadata to improve description and retrieval of Nordic Internet resources (Hakala et al., 1998). The Dublin Core was

Figure 2.5

The Dublin Core Element Set

Title: Name of resource

Creator: Entity primarily responsible for content

Subject: Topic (keywords, controlled terms, classification)

Description: Abstract, contents, annotation

Publisher: Entity responsible for making resource available

Contributor: Entity which has made significant contributions to content

Date: Date associated with event in life cycle of resource

Type: Genre or nature of content

Format: File type or physical nature

Identifier: Unique identification (e.g., the URL)

Source: Reference to the resource from which this was derived

Language: Language of the intellectual content

Relation: Reference to a related resource

Coverage: Extent, scope (e.g., spatial, temporal, jurisdictional characteristics)

Rights: Information about rights associated with resource

Figure 2.6

Embedded Dublin Core Metadata

```
<!DOCTYPE html PUBLIC "-//W3C//DTD XHTML 1.0
transitional//EN" "DTD/xhtml1-transitional.dtd">

<html xmlns="http://www.w3.org/1999/xhtml" xml:lang="en"
lang="en"

<head>

<title>LIS 415, Organization of Knowledge in Libraries, Course
Page</title>

<link rel="schema.DC" href="http://purl.org/DC/elements/1.1" />
<meta name="DC.Creator" content="Schwartz, Candy" />
<meta name="DC.Title" content="Course page—LIS 415" />
<meta name="DC.Subject" content="Cataloging" />
<meta name="DC.Description" content="Main page for course in
organization of information, cataloguing, classification." />
<meta name="DC.Publisher" content="Simmons College" />
<meta name="DC.Type" content="Text" />
<meta name="DC.Format" content="text/html" />
<meta name="DC.Identifier"
content="http://web.simmons.edu/~schwartz/415.html" />

</head>

<body>
... [Content displayed by browser] ...
</body>

</html>
```

selected following an evaluation of over 20 different metadata formats, and work over the next two years generated an interactive Dublin Core template (see Figure 2.7), a Dublin Core-to-MARC converter, user guides, and various other tools. The project is now continuing as Nordic Metadata II, and will include refinement of the components of the toolkit as well as support for XML and the Resource Description Framework (RDF), both of which are discussed below.

THE MLs

Markup languages are coding systems used to "mark up" text and other documentary contents so that they can be transmitted, processed, and rendered across different machine platforms. Markup languages generally cover descriptive information (e.g., this is a title, this is an address), or procedural information (e.g., this should be emphasized, this should be centered). The markup languages prevalent on the Web use angular brackets around element tags which are in plain text to encode document content. Browsers or other receiving systems then interpret the code and render or manipulate the content according to instructions embedded in the browser, or according to programmed instructions regarding disposition of the coded elements.

Although HTML is currently the standard for presenting Web documents, other markup languages have gained prominence in the public eye, and two in particular are important in any consideration of metadata: the older parent of markup, Standard Generalized Markup Language (SGML) and the new kid on the block, XML.

HyperText Markup Language (HTML)

Most of us are familiar with HTML, the publishing language used to encode materials for document presentation on the World Wide Web. HTML was developed by Tim Berners-Lee to facilitate creation of Web documents, and has gone through various editions as the Web has evolved. In early 2000, HTML 4 was reformatted in XML so that properly coded documents would be able to be inte-

Figure 2.7

Dublin Core Template, Nordic Metadata Project

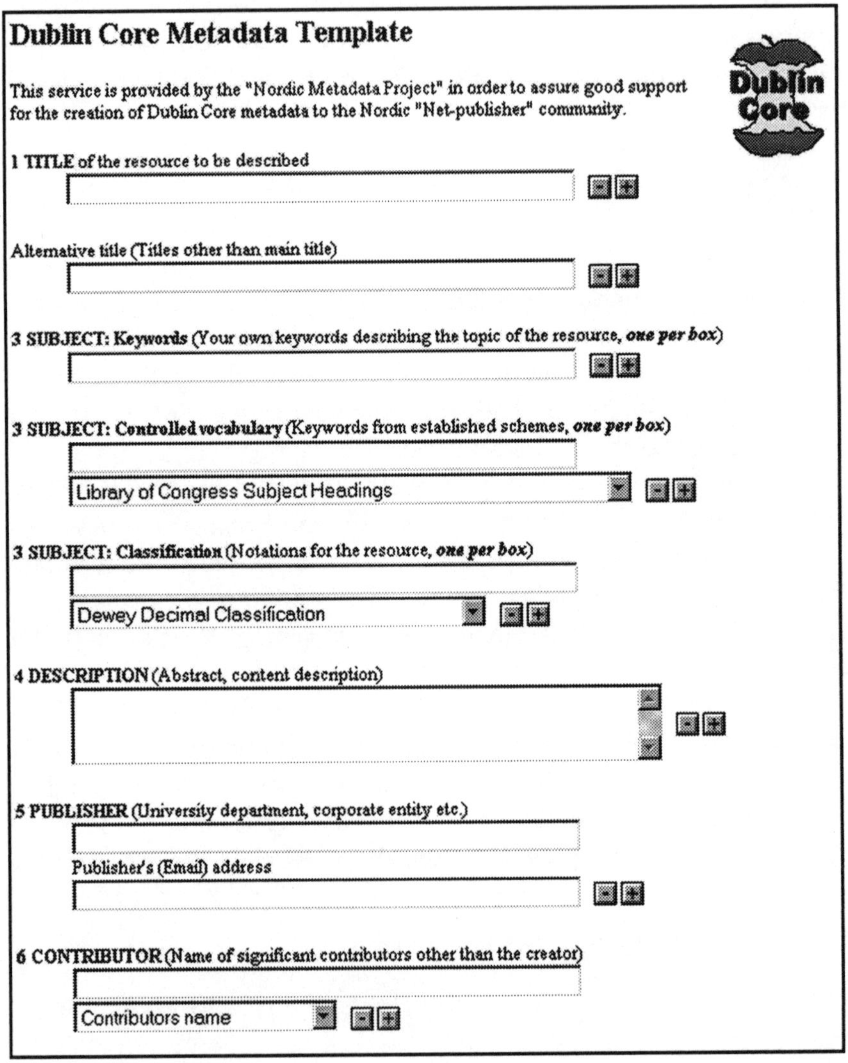

Dublin Core Metadata Template

This service is provided by the "Nordic Metadata Project" in order to assure good support for the creation of Dublin Core metadata to the Nordic "Net-publisher" community.

1 TITLE of the resource to be described

Alternative title (Titles other than main title)

3 SUBJECT: Keywords (Your own keywords describing the topic of the resource, *one per box*)

3 SUBJECT: Controlled vocabulary (Keywords from established schemes, *one per box*)

Library of Congress Subject Headings

3 SUBJECT: Classification (Notations for the resource, *one per box*)

Dewey Decimal Classification

4 DESCRIPTION (Abstract, content description)

5 PUBLISHER (University department, corporate entity etc.)

Publisher's (Email) address

6 CONTRIBUTOR (Name of significant contributors other than the creator)

Contributors name

Reprinted with permission of Juha Hakala, Library Network Services, Helsinki University Library.

grated into XML applications. The resulting current W3C specification is the XHTML 1.0 Recommendation, with XHTML 1.1 in the works (World Wide Web Consortium, 2000a). XHTML uses the same elements and attributes as HTML 4 but has more stringent requirements for their use in creating a well-formed document (World Wide Web Consortium, 2000a).

All W3C HTML specifications have included the META element, for marking up information identifying properties of a document, such as author, keywords describing its content, and so on. META elements are coded within the HEAD element, which contains constituents which are not part of displayable content, such as TITLE, META, and so on. The HTML 4 specification expands on previous versions with a wealth of examples of the use of the META element, including Dublin Core applications. HTML 4 also includes the PROFILE attribute of the HEAD element for specifying the location of a metadata profile, the LINK element, which conveys inter-document relationships, and the SCHEME attribute of the META element, which can be used to provide context for interpreting metadata (e.g., <meta name="DC.subject" scheme="LCSH" content="Classification">).

Apart from what information a page creator might have chosen to identify with META tags, XHTML elements are deficient with respect to identifying the meaningful structure of a document. Elements which identify title, headings, and subheadings are present, but the majority of elements are concerned with presentation structure (paragraph, lists, tables, and so on) rather than content. This renders XHTML unsuitable as a metadata standard by itself, although it can certainly serve as a carrier of metadata, as was seen earlier in Figure 2.6. Also, XHTML is not extensible—new elements are added after a lengthy process of standards revision.

Standard Generalized Markup Language (SGML)

SGML evolved from efforts in the 1960s to develop ways to code structural elements into machine-readable documents so that they could be exchanged and processed across systems. IBM's Generalized Markup Language (GML) and the Graphic Communications

Association's GenCode formed the basis for what became the international standard ISO 8879, SGML (Alschuler, 1995).

SGML is a language which is used to create markup languages (the markup language HTML, for example, is actually an application of SGML). An SGML document consist of three parts:

- The SGML declaration, which defines the document character set, name lengths for elements, and other basic parameters;

- The document type definition (DTD), which is the syntax defining the element set, element attributes, and other features of the structure of the class of documents to which this one belongs; and

- The document instance, that is, the actual document, marked up according to the structure defined in the DTD. Figure 2.8 shows an extremely simple SGML DTD and marked-up document.

SGML is a descriptive language rather than a procedural one. That is, SGML provides for identifying what something is (this string of text is a "title," for example) rather than the how it should be processed or displayed (e.g., put this string of text in italics). Depending on the application, procedural information for an SGML document may come from other sources (typically style sheets). The current XHTML specification evidences a return to its SGML origins through the deprecation of many procedural elements and attributes (all font elements, for example) in favor of style sheets.

SGML has been used widely in the publishing community for decades, and many SGML applications have been developed. Three which are of particular interest in the domain of bibliographic resource description are the TEI Header, the EAD, and XML, which has been described as SGML "lite."

Text Encoding Initiative (TEI)

The initiative for the TEI came in 1987 from communities concerned with coding electronic texts for scholarly research—specifi-

Figure 2.8

Simple SGML DTD and Document Instance

```
<!DOCTYPE speech [
<!ELEMENT speech - - (title?, speaker?, sentence+) >
<!ELEMENT title - 0 (#PCDATA) >
<!ELEMENT speaker - 0 (#PCDATA) >
<!ELEMENT sentence - - (#PCDATA) >
]>

<speech>

   <title>Welcome to New Students</title>

   <speaker>Jim Matarazzo</speaker>

   <sentence>Welcome to the Graduate School of Library and
   Information Science.</sentence>

   <sentence>This is a very exciting time to enter the field, and the
   faculty and staff look forward to helping you in any way we
   can.</sentence>

   <sentence>Your faculty advisor will meet with you over lunch
   today to discuss your course choices, and then we would like you
   to take the library orientation tour.</sentence>

   <sentence>I will now turn the program over to Dr. Schwartz, who
   will introduce the program of study.</sentence>

<speech>
```

cally the Association for Computational Linguistics, the Association for Computers and the Humanities, and the Association for Computational Linguistics. SGML was chosen as the basis for the TEI because it offered the best combination of flexibility and (relative) simplicity and was seen as an accepted standard. The TEI Consortium, responsible for maintenance and revision, was established in 1999, and that same year saw a celebration of the tenth birthday of the TEI in a special issue of *Computers and the Humanities*, showing proof of its acceptance and popularity.

The TEI DTD, or family of DTDs, is modular in nature, incorporating core sets of elements applicable to all documents, base sets which are applicable to texts of specific kinds (e.g., drama or verse), and element sets for additional features, such as critical apparatus, or meta-information about the coding (Barnard & Ide, 1997). A TEILITE DTD has been issued, using a subset of TEI elements, but still offering sophistication in markup. The Electronic Text Center at the University of Virginia and the Center for Electronic Texts in the Humanities at Rutgers University are both examples of rich collections of TEI-encoded texts, and both are actively engaged in EAD and XML applications as well.

All TEI documents are required to have a TEI Header (TEIH), which consists of four sections: a file description (containing bibliographical elements similar to descriptive cataloging), an encoding description (describing aspects of the transition from uncoded to coded text), a text profile (characterizing subject and context), and a revision history (relating changes in the electronic text). Figure 2.9 illustrates the TEI Header content. Portions of the TEIH metadata can logically serve as the document representation for retrieval purposes. In terms of library cataloging, interactions between TEIH and MARC are problematic (Barry, 1998; Giordano, 1994; Palowitch & Horowitz, 1996), but several interesting reports on this and related topics appear in papers from a conference on *TEI and XML in Digital Libraries* (1998).

Encoded Archival Description (EAD)

In 1993, as principal investigator for a project at the University of California, Berkeley, Daniel Pitti began work on developing a stan-

Figure 2.9

TEI Header Content

```
<teiHeader>

  <fileDesc>
    Bibliographic description of the file (creator, title, publisher,
    extent, etc.) and the printed source.
  </fileDesc>

  <encodingDesc>
    Details about the coding of the file.
  </encodingDesc>

  <profileDesc>
    Description of non-bibliographic elements, such as language,
    genre, subject contents (including controlled terms and
    classification), and so on.
  </profileDesc>

  <revisionDesc>
    Information about revisions and changes to the file.
  </revisionDesc>

</teiHeader>
```

dard for encoding archival finding aids. Finding aids are descriptions of archival collections, usually containing supplementary material related to the subject and context of the collection, as well as inventories and registers. Obviously a nonproprietary coding standard would greatly enhance access to archival resource information over the Internet. Pitti's (1999) overview of the EAD includes an introduction to the differences between archival and library resource description needs and points out why a new standard was necessary. Following several years of research and revision, and in consultation with national and international archival communities, the EAD DTD was established, and is now maintained at the Library of Congress, in partnership with the Society of American Archivists.

The EAD consists of three major sections: the EAD Header (citation and record creation information, modeled on the TEIH), Front Matter (for holding local "title page," dedication, or other prefatory material), and the Archival Description (the information about the archive, including a substantial collection of elements designed to promote access through controlled vocabulary terms). The Online Archive of California, part of the California Digital Library, includes the finding aids of more than 50 different institutions, searchable through one interface. Queries can make use of Boolean operators, proximity, and truncation, and can be run through several collections at once. Individual finding aids are displayed with expandable tables of contents for ease of perusal (see Figure 2.10). This project offers a fine example of the benefits derived from taking advantage of the structure afforded by SGML.

eXtensible Markup Language (XML)

Why has XML attracted so much attention, not only in library-land but also in the worlds of e-commerce, e-publishing, and the Internet industry? For reasons outlined above, HTML is unsuitable for access and retrieval, but HTML documents are universally accessible to Web browsers. SGML applications such as the TEI and EAD support access and retrieval, but general browsers require special readers or plug-ins to read SGML documents (for that reason, many TEI and EAD projects serve SGML documents as HTML for

Figure 2.10

EAD Application, Online Archive of California

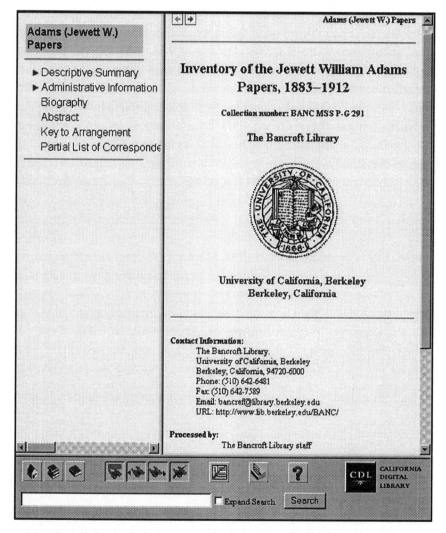

Adams (Jewett W.) Papers

- ► Descriptive Summary
- ► Administrative Information
- Biography
- Abstract
- Key to Arrangement
- Partial List of Corresponde

Adams (Jewett W.) Papers

Inventory of the Jewett William Adams Papers, 1883–1912

Collection number: BANC MSS P-G 291

The Bancroft Library

University of California, Berkeley
Berkeley, California

Contact Information:
The Bancroft Library.
University of California, Berkeley
Berkeley, California, 94720-6000
Phone: (510) 642-6481
Fax: (510) 642-7589
Email: bancref@library.berkeley.edu
URL: http://www.lib.berkeley.edu/BANC/

Processed by:
The Bancroft Library staff

CDL CALIFORNIA DIGITAL LIBRARY

☐ Expand Search   Search

presentation to users, thus preserving structural advantages, such as fielded search, while allowing easy access to search results). XML hopes to offer the best of both worlds—a simplified version of SGML, so that the option of structuring data is available to a wider audience, and readability through general browsers (or at least the latest versions of them).

Like SGML, XML is a metalanguage for defining markup, and permits the creation of DTDs. Unlike SGML, XML documents are not *required* to have an explicit DTD, although the structure enabled through tagging will be more useful and interpretable in the presence of a DTD. XML 1.0 was posted as a W3C Recommendation early in 1998, and associated standards in development encompass query languages, style sheets, and syntaxes for new kinds of hyperlinking.

According to the W3C, XML will:

- Enable internationalized media-independent electronic publishing;
- Allow industries to define platform-independent protocols for the exchange of data, especially the data of electronic commerce;
- Deliver information to user agents in a form that allows automatic processing after receipt;
- Make it easy for people to process data using inexpensive software;
- Allow people to display information the way they want it; and
- Provide metadata—data about information—that will help people find information and help information producers and consumers find each other. (Connolly & Bray, 1999)

While this may appear to be ambitious, XML has emerged as a powerful tool in resource description and communication. Being based on SGML, standards such as EAD and TEI are also XML-compliant (with some modification, since XML is a reduction of SGML). The

Library of Congress and others have worked on SGML DTDs for MARC and MARC-to-SGML conversion, and similar projects are underway for MARC and XML.

The EAD, TEI, and MARC are examples of metadata standards whose element sets have been agreed upon by the communities whose interests they serve. Sharing and integration of XML resources described by these element sets is not without problems, but at least the meaning of particular elements is documented. However, in an XML environment, a foreign document can include an element set which is unknown to a receiving system. While the tagging might convey that there is, for example, an element called NAME, this does not say anything about what NAME means or how it should be interpreted or processed. The potential exists for the development of thousands of local DTDs, possibly many which are being used for the same type of data. A local DTD is acceptable when resources are being used within a locally controlled set of applications, but in cooperative resource sharing it inhibits resource representation and retrieval. The Resource Description Framework (RDF) and the use of namespaces address these problems.

RDF and Namespaces

The RDF is a W3C initiative and an official Recommendation. RDF provides a data model in which metadata can be associated with a resource by declaring values for various property types of that resource (e.g., creator="Schwartz, Candy") where the property types are associated with one or more schemas which define the property types and their attributes. XML is used as the syntax to enable that association, and the XML namespace facility is the method by which the location of the property information is specified. Figure 2.11 illustrates these basic concepts (for amplification, see Iannella's [1998] *Idiot's Guide*). The difference between a DTD and a schema is that a DTD specifies what elements are allowable (i.e., what properties are identified) and how they are constrained with respect to use in marking up a document, while a schema provides information about interpreting the properties—so, for example, a schema might constrain the values of a property. The Dublin Core

Figure 2.11

XML, RDF, and Namespaces

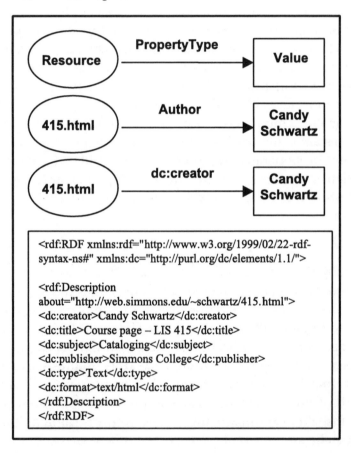

is an example of a schema. A working group of the W3C is developing a schema language which will replace the XML DTD and extend the capabilities of XML in the RDF model (Ioannides, 2000).

In the RDF model, different types of metadata, emanating from different agencies for different purposes, can interoperate (this concept was presaged by the Warwick Framework, an outcome of work on the Dublin Core). Assuming well-developed schemata, all sorts of possibilities follow. The W3C identifies a number of practical uses of RDF, including thesauri and classification schemes, Web site maps, Web page content descriptions, management of privacy practices, descriptions of device capabilities, rating systems, and digital signature management (World Wide Web Consortium, 2000b).

OCLC's CORC project applies RDF and XML namespaces to CORC resources. In fact, CORC resources can be viewed in MARC, Dublin Core, Dublin Core HTML, and Dublin Core RDF (see Figure 2.12). CORC is a particularly interesting example of RDF because of its content and richness, but there are many RDF applications in development currently, and there will be many more as the W3C standards evolve and as different communities develop metadata applications.

A WORK IN (RAPID) PROGRESS

Although it may appear complicated, technical, and overburdened with acronyms, the application of metadata to networked resources has brought a new level of excitement to resource description, and metadata standards development has made possible a wealth of opportunities for resource sharing and interoperability. This chapter has highlighted only some of the better known "bibliographic" metadata projects—the interested reader should be aware that there are many more. Some of the most long-standing among these are:

- Internet Anonymous FTP Archives (IAFA) templates, used by the Resource Organisation and Discovery in Subject-based Services (ROADS) Project as a basis for cataloging Internet resources in subject gateways;

Figure 2.12

CORC Resource View Options

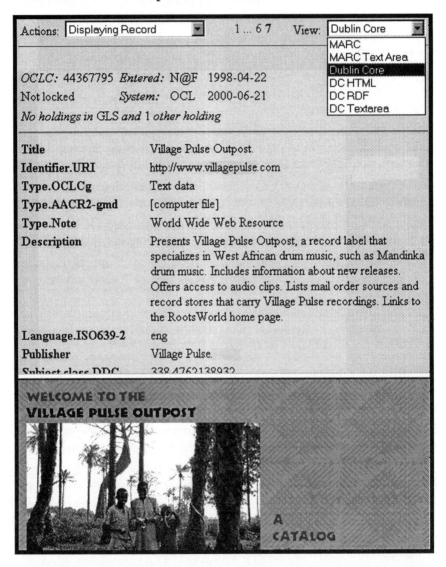

- The Government Information Locator Service (GILS), a Federal Information Processing Standard which includes approved core metadata for government information;
- The Content Standard for Digital Geospatial Metadata (CSDGM), developed by the Federal Geographic Data Committee (FGDC) for describing geographic data; and
- Categories for the Description of Works of Art (CDWA), an initiative of the Art Information Task Force (AITF).

Current work in metadata across the bibliographic community, including most of the approaches covered in this chapter, focuses on:

- Making metadata standards work with SGML and XML and in the RDF model;
- Developing toolkits (record templates, parsers, etc.);
- Coordinating and expanding user communities;
- Establishing registries for metadata applications; and
- Establishing cross-system conversion and mapping capabilities (e.g., TEIH to MARC, DC to MARC).

Considering this last point, metadata can act as a *lingua franca* for unified interaction with independent (and distributed) resource collections which use different access points. Lynch (1998) suggests this federating role for the Dublin Core.

Direct conversion between formats for the purposes of reducing data entry effort can be problematic when the conventions of data entry differ. For example, a conversion algorithm could pull some information from, say, a TEI Header into a MARC record with relatively little difficulty. If the purpose of the conversion is to add a representation of the e-text into an existing library catalog, the fields in the converted MARC record will have been populated by information which well may not conform to the authorities used for description (and especially for access) in the rest of the catalog. Alternatively, there may be differences between two standards in the way a field of information is fragmented. Gains in richness of coverage may be at the sacrifice of retrieval performance.

Most metadata standards have been developed by groups of experts for application in a specific domain. In 1996, Heery suggested that:

> It is unlikely that one format will satisfy the requirements of all stakeholders. Different disciplines and professional backgrounds favour different approaches to resource description; different navigation and searching tools favour different record formats. So it would seem that, at least in the short term, there will be an increasing need for interoperability between different systems based on different metadata. (p. 371)

Metadata tools, such as XML and the RDF, and query management tools, such as Z39.50, have been key elements in promoting interoperability and the coexistence of a plurality of metadata approaches.

The remainder of this book will be concerned not with how description is stored (the container) and handled (delivery), but rather with what constitutes description (content), and especially subject description.

REFERENCES

Alschuler, Liora. (1995). *ABCD–SGML: A user's guide to structured information*. Boston: International Thomson.

Baca, Murtha (Ed.). (1998). *Introduction to metadata: Pathways to digital information*. Los Angeles: J. Paul Getty Trust.

Barnard, David T., & Ide, Nancy M. (1997). The Text Encoding Initiative: Flexible and extensible document encoding. *Journal of the American Society for Information Science, 48*, 622–628.

Barry, Randall. (1998, June 30). *Descriptive metadata: The TEI Header, MARC, and AACR2*. Retrieved May 20, 1999 from the World Wide Web: http://www.hti.umich.edu/misc/ssp/workshops/teidlf/barry.html.

Bosak, Jon, & Bray, Tim. (1999). XML and the second-generation Web. *Scientific American, 280*(5). Retrieved November 24, 1999 from the World Wide Web: http://www.scientificamerican.com/1999/0599issue/0599bosak.html.

Burnett, Kathleen, Ng, Kwong Bor, & Park, Soyeaon. (1999). A comparison of the two traditions of metadata development. *Journal of the American Society for Information Science, 50,* 1209–1217.

Caplan, Priscilla. (1995). You call it corn, we call it syntax-independent metadata for document-like objects. *Public-Access Computer Systems Review, 6*(4). Retrieved July 26, 1998 from the World Wide Web: http://info.lib.uh.edu/pr/v6/n4/capl6n4.html.

Connolly, Dan, & Bray, Tim. (1999, November 26). *Extensible Markup Language (XML) activity.* Retrieved November 27, 1999 from the World Wide Web: http://www.w3.org/XML/Activity.html.

Cutter, Charles Ammi. (1904). *Rules for a dictionary catalog* (4th ed.). Washington, DC: U.S. GPO.

Dempsey, Lorcan, & Heery, Rachel. (1998). Metadata: A current view of practice and issues. *Journal of Documentation, 54,* 145–173.

Dempsey, Lorcan, Russell, Rosemary, & Heery, Rachel. (1997, November 17). *In at the shallow end: Metadata and cross-domain resource discovery* (Arts and Humanities Data Service, Discovering Online Resources). Retrieved November 30, 1999 from the World Wide Web: http://ahds.ac.uk/public/metadata/disc_07.html.

Gaynor, Edward. (1996). *From MARC to markup: SGML and online library systems.* Retrieved July 26, 1998 from the World Wide Web: http://www.lib.virginia.edu/speccol/scdc/articles/alcts_brief.html.

Giordano, Richard. (1994). The documentation of electronic texts using Text Encoding Initiative headers: An introduction. *Library Resources & Technical Services, 38,* 389–401.

Guenther, Rebecca S. (1994). The challenges of electronic texts in the library: Bibliographic control and access. In B. Sutton (Ed.), *Library texts in an electronic age: Scholarly implications and library services: 1994 proceedings of the Data Processing Clinic* (pp. 149–172). Urbana, IL: Graduate School of Library and Information Science, University of Illinois at Urbana–Champaign.

Hakala, Juha, Hansen, Preben, Husby, Ole, Koch, Traugott, & Thorborg, Susanne. (1998, July). *The Nordic metadata project.* Retrieved November 25, 1999 from the World Wide Web: http://linnea.helsinki.fi/meta/nmfinal.htm.

Heery, Rachel. (1996). Review of metadata formats. *Program, 30,* 345–373.

Hopkins, Judith. (1999). USMARC as a metadata shell. *Journal of Internet Cataloging, 2*(1), 55–69.

Hudgins, Jean, Agnew, Grace, & Brown, Elizabeth. (1999). *Getting mileage out of metadata.* Chicago: American Library Association (LITA guides #5).

Ianella, Renato. (1998). An idiot's guide to the Resource Description Framework. *New Review of Information Networking, 4,* 181–188.

Ioannides, Demetrios. (2000). XML schema languages: Beyond DTD. *Library Hi Tech, 18*(1), 9–14.

Koch, Traugott. (2000). Quality-controlled subject gateways; Definitions, typologies, empirical overview. *Online Information Review, 24,* 24–34.

Lange, Holley R., & Winkler, B. Jean. (1997). Taming the Internet: Metadata, a work in progress. *Advances in Librarianship, 21,* 47–72.

Lynch, Clifford. (1998, February 27). The Dublin Core descriptive metadata program: Strategic implications for libraries and networked information access. *ARL, 196.* Retrieved October 16, 1998 from the World Wide Web: http://www.arl.org/newsltr/196/dublin.html.

Milstead, Jessica, & Feldman, Susan. (1999a). Metadata. *Online, 23*(1), 32–40.

Milstead, Jessica, & Feldman, Susan. (1999b). Metadata: Cataloging by any other name. *Online, 23*(1), 25–31.

Mitchell, Steve, & Mooney, Margaret. (1996). INFOMINE: A model Web-based academic virtual library. *Information Technology & Libraries, 15*(1), 20–25.

Olson, Nancy (Ed.). (1997). Cataloging Internet resources (2nd ed.). Dublin, OH: OCLC, Inc. Retrieved May 20, 1998 from the World Wide Web: http://www.purl.org/oclc/cataloging-internet/.

Open eBook Authoring Group. (1999, September 16). *Open eBook&trade publication structure 1.0.* Retrieved November 25, 1999 from the World Wide Web: http://www.openebook.org/OEB1.html.

Palowitch, Casey, & Horowitz, Lisa. (1996). Meta-information structures for networked information resources. *Cataloging & Classification Quarterly, 21*(3/4), 109–130.

Pitti, Daniel. (1999, November). Encoded Archival Description: An introduction and overview. *D-Lib Magazine, 5*(11). Retrieved November 29, 1999 from the World Wide Web: http://www.dlib.org/dlib/november99/11pitti.html.

Powell, Andy. (1997, July 16). Dublin Core management. *Ariadne, 10*. Retrieved July 26, 1998 from the World Wide Web: http://www.ariadne.ac.uk/issue10/dublin/.Metadata Management.

Sha, Vianne T. (1995). Cataloguing Internet resources: The library approach. *Electronic Library, 13*, 467–476.

Taylor, Arlene G. (1999). Where does AACR2 fall short for Internet resources? *Journal of Internet Cataloging, 2*(2), 43–50.

TEI and XML in Digital Libraries. (1998). Retrieved November 25, 1999 from the World Wide Web: http://www.hti.umich.edu/misc/ssp/workshops/teidlf/.

Vellucci, Sherry L. (1996). Herding cats: Options for organizing Internet resources. *Internet Reference Services Quarterly, 1*(4), 9–30.

Vellucci, Sherry L. (1999). Metadata. *Annual Review of Information Science & Technology, 33*, 187–222.

Weibel, Stuart L. (1995, July). Metadata: The foundations of resource description. *D-Lib Magazine*. Retrieved May 14, 1999 from the World Wide Web: http://www.dlib.org/dlib/July95/07weibel.html.

Weibel, Stuart. (1997). The Dublin Core: A simple content description model for electronic resources. *Bulletin of the American Society for Information Science, 24*(1), 9–11.

World Wide Web Consortium. (2000a, August 25). *Hypertext Markup Language home page*. Retrieved August 25, 2000 from the World Wide Web: http://www.w3.org/MarkUp/.

World Wide Web Consortium. (2000b, May 8). *Metadata activity statement*. Retrieved August 25, 2000 from the World Wide Web: http://www.w3.org/ Metadata/Activity.html.

WEB PAGE

Metadata Resources. http://www.simmons.edu/~schwartz/mymeta.html.

3

Classification

Library classification schemes generally place books on similar subjects near each other on the shelves, or catalog entries near each other in the card drawer or on the screen of the OPAC. This affords users the opportunity of browsing the collection. Displaying Internet resources in a systematic topical arrangement has the same effect. Some of the most popular Internet search services focus on classification and categorization (e.g., Yahoo and LookSmart). Even those services which concentrate on providing word-searching capabilities often offer browseable categories as well (e.g., InfoSeek or Lycos). For the user who is attempting to "see what's out there," a subject arrangement is especially useful. It takes a large, disorganized collection of resources and breaks it into smaller scannable groups of items related to each other topically.

Systematic arrangements can be created ad hoc, based on the collection content at a point in time, and then revised as the collection grows. Alternatively, they can draw from existing library devices, notably library classification schemes. The categories and classes in a systematic arrangement, whatever the basis, can be expressed alphabetically, notationally (i.e., using classification numbers), or graphically and can form the basis for three-dimensional browsing systems.

BACKGROUND

There is an infinite number of ways to arrange things by their subject content. However, libraries (and other information services) have been developing and applying classification schemes for well over a century. The general history, principles, and application of major library classification schemes are well documented in introductory and advanced texts and readers in cataloging and classification, such as Carpenter and Svenonius (1985), Chan (1994, 1999), Chan, Comaromi, Mitchell, and Satija (1996), McIlwaine (1995a), Painter (1972), and Taylor (1999, 2000).

Using an existing classification scheme to arrange Internet resources has some obvious advantages in a library setting:

- Users are familiar with the scheme through its use for the library collection;
- In an integrated OPAC environment, Internet resources will be described in the same way as other items represented in the catalog and will be searchable using the same tools;
- Creating and maintaining a new classification scheme is difficult and prohibitively expensive; and
- Staff are already trained in the principles of applying the classification scheme.

Library classification schemes are not perfect. Since a book can generally only be placed in one location, library classification schemes are designed to provide the "best" location, based on someone's viewpoint when the scheme was created. For example, under the most popular general library classification schemes, books about cataloging maps would be classified with books on cataloging rather than with books on maps. Each scheme reflects a set of decisions about which collocations are useful. To some degree this can be overcome in an online environment, as Internet resources are not "shelved" and can certainly be classified in several places (bending the "rules" of using the classification scheme).

Some library classification schemes lend themselves to browseability in an online environment, and others do not. The utility of a specific classification scheme for Internet resources generally relates to the number of resources being organized, the structure of the scheme, and how the site manager chooses to apply it.

One approach is to use a simple, broad classification, with perhaps two or three levels of hierarchy. This might be extracted from the top levels of a full library classification, or it might be constructed for the purpose at hand. A simple classification might suffice for subarranging several hundred resources into groups small enough to be amenable to browsing, but would not be useful if the collection were many thousands of items large.

Since one of the desired results of classifying Internet resources is to present small scannable groups of related items, the larger the collection, the more hierarchically rich the classification has to be. On the other hand, an overly rich hierarchy can result in "groups" of one or two, which is not terribly helpful for browsing. The flexibility of the online environment, however, can overcome this problem by letting users examine just the resources classified at one specific level, or all resources classified at one level and all of its subhierarchical levels. Several of the projects discussed below have taken this approach, which allows for resources to be assigned detailed classification without imposing very small groupings on the browsing process. This has the added advantage of adapting to growth as the collection of Internet resources gets larger (which it inevitably will). It also means that the level of detail in classifying Internet resources can be the same as that used in classifying library holdings, which promotes coherence in an integrated catalog.

A classification scheme may be topically detailed but hierarchically "flat," meaning that the classification represents many narrow subjects under a broad class without an intervening hierarchical breakdown (see Figure 3.1). This is not effective as a browsing tool as it results in very small groups, classified under specific topics, without the available structure for creating larger groupings at higher

Figure 3.1

Different Degrees of Hierarchy

Foodstuffs	Foodstuffs	Foodstuffs
Apples	Bread	Bread
Asparagus	Bagels	Bagels
Bagels	Fruit	Fruit
Carrots	Apples	Berries
Lemons	Lemons	Raspberries
Lima Beans	Oranges	Citrus Fruits
Oranges	Pears	Lemons
Pears	Raspberries	Oranges
Pecans	Nuts	Pomaceous Fruits
Raspberries	Pecans	Apples
Spinach	Walnuts	Pears
Walnuts	Vegetables	Nuts
	Asparagus	Pecans
	Carrots	Walnuts
	Lima Beans	Vegetables
	Spinach	Root Vegetables
		Carrots
		Leafy Greens
		Asparagus
		Legumes
		Lima Beans
		Cooking Greens
		Spinach
Alphabetical list—the longer it gets, the harder it is to scan.	*Somewhat better organized—but still a problem if list gets longer.*	*Systematic listing—can accommodate new additions without as much loss of scannability.*

hierarchical levels. The three most popular general library classifications are the Dewey Decimal Classification (DDC, or Dewey), the Library of Congress Classification (LCC), and the Universal Decimal Classification (UDC). Each has been used in Internet applications. There are also many subject-specific classification schemes, typically developed by publishers of indexing and abstracting services. Some of these have been used as well.

Kwasnik (1999) provides an excellent overview of four types of classification—hierarchies, trees, paradigms, and faceted analysis—providing for each a consideration of structural requirements, strengths, and limitations. Most general and subject-specific classification schemes fall into the hierarchies category and are enumerative—that is, each notational string in the classification scheme represents a predetermined combination of topics built into the number (see Dewey example in Figure 3.2). Faceted classification schemes take a different approach—the scheme presents isolated elements of notation representing individual topics rather than preset combinations. The coordination of topics for a specific item using a faceted classification is accomplished by combining the notational elements according to a set of rules (see Figure 3.3). Historically, the faceted approach has been restricted to a very few library classification schemes, although it is widely used as a method of constructing thesauri for indexing applications. Some enumerative schemes do contain elements of faceted classification—UDC is a hybrid of the two, and Dewey displays some facet elements in its notation.

The faceted approach has advantages in an electronic environment. The notational string contains the complete notational "bit" for each topic and can be deconstructed for purposes of rearrangement (and retrieval). This would not be as easily done with LCC, as the notation is not "expressive"—the letter/number combinations do not reflect the hierarchy in which the subject stands.

Most library classifications are now machine-readable, which means that the words and phrases which express the subject of the notation are available for manipulation. In fact, it might be possible to translate LCC numbers into their text equivalents, and identify facets in that manner, but for structural reasons it would probably not be very successful. Dewey and UDC, on the other hand, lend

Figure 3.2

Topical Order: Example from Dewey

025.3414076   A workbook on subject cataloging of manuscripts

02   Library and information sciences

  5   Operations of libraries, archives, information centers

    3   Bibliographical analysis and control

      4   Subject analysis and control

        1   Manuscripts, archival materials, rarities

          4   Manuscripts

            07   Education, research, related topics

              6   Programmed texts

Figure 3.3

Faceted Classification

Library and Information Science

A/C	General aspects	
A		Forms of presentation
Adh		**Programmed texts**

[D/E	Subfields of LIS in general
F/G	Users
H/K	Library types and systems]

L/O	Library materials	
Mb/Me	Unpublished	
Me		**Archival materials**

P/W	Operations and agents	
S/W	Technical operations	
T	Information retrieval	
VB	Non-subject indexing	
Vdb		**Descriptive cataloging**

Vdb-Me-Adh   A workbook on cataloging archival materials

Based loosely on the classification scheme developed by Daniel and Mills (1975).

themselves to this approach. Some of the projects discussed below use the verbal manifestations in place of, or as well as, the notation. Another advantage to incorporating text representations of notation is the addition of terminology for query-based retrieval.

All of the examples discussed below use classification. They differ with respect to:

- Choice of classification scheme;
- Representation of Internet resources (especially whether or not the resources are maintained in a local file, with descriptive metadata information);
- Level of hierarchical detail;
- Whether the entire classification scheme is presented or only those topics at which resources are gathered (the former results in a more logical navigation, but empty categories);
- Method of display (especially notation versus text); and
- Devices for navigating the classification.

A Word About ROADS

Resource Organisation and Discovery in Subject-based Services (ROADS) software is not a classification scheme implementation, but a means to the use of classification on the Internet. ROADS provides a set of tools for creating and maintaining metadata records in subject gateways. The metadata formats are based on IAFA templates, from which ROADS can derive HTML pages for browsing and access, including browsing classification hierarchies. ROADS does not require the use of specific tools for subject access, and so various of the ROADS applications use UDC, DDC, or other classification schemes. ROADS creation is part of the Electronic Libraries Programme (eLib) supported by the Joint Information Systems Committee (JISC), a body formed by national U.K. higher education funding agencies. Beginning in the mid-1990s, eLib funded the development of a number of subject-specialized gateways to scholarly networked resources. This in turn led to the establishment of the still-emerging Resource Discovery Network (RDN), which serves as a gateway to gateways. Various eLib and ROADS-based gateways are described in more detail in this and other chapters of this book.

Gateways which implement all or part of ROADS include:

- ADAM (Art, Design, Architecture and Media);
- ALEX (a collection of electronic texts);
- BeCal (Belief, Culture and Learning);
- Biz/ed (business and economics);
- EELS (Engineering Electronic Library, Sweden);
- The Finnish Virtual Library project;
- HISTORY;
- NADIR (a German political information magazine and gateway);
- NOVAGate (a Nordic gateway to information on forestry and veterinary and agricultural sciences);
- OMNI (Organising Medical Networked Information);
- PORT (The U.K. National Maritime Museum's Internet catalog);
- ROUTES (Resources for Open University Teachers and Students);
- SOSIG (Social Science Information Gateway); and
- Wastewater Engineering Virtual Library.

DEWEY ON THE WEB

First published in 1876 and now in its twenty-first edition, the Dewey Decimal Classification has appeared in more than 30 languages and is the most widely used library classification in the world (*A Brief Introduction to the Dewey Decimal Classification*, 1998). Forest Press, a division of OCLC, publishes full and abridged editions, special issues for specific sections or communities, and a CD-ROM version, *Dewey for Windows*. Dewey is also accessible under OCLC's CORC project (described in Chapter 2). Classification specialists in LC's Decimal Classification Division add Dewey subject numbers to over 110,000 USMARC records annually, an activity which is valuable for users of USMARC records and which also allows electronic Dewey products to exploit the relationships among Dewey numbers and LC subject headings. OCLC's Office of Research has incorporated Dewey into many of its advanced efforts in the areas of online public access catalogs and Internet cataloging.

Dewey is eminently hierarchical, with a numeric and "expressive" notation (i.e., the numbers reflect the hierarchical position of a topic) which can be easily abridged for settings where full, detailed classification is undesirable. As might be expected from a classification scheme with the word "decimal" in its title, Dewey starts with 10 main classes, each of which has 10 divisions, each of which (with some exceptions) has 10 sections, and so on (see Figure 3.4). In addition to assigning numbers from the schedules (the main layout of subjects in the classification schemes), classifiers build numbers by appending notation from tables (either of common application or specific to a subject area) or (less frequently) by following instructions which lead to combining numbers from different parts of the schedules. Notation is expressed as a number between 000 and 999, going to a potentially almost infinite number of decimal places. Since the same tables are used throughout Dewey, and since there is consistency in arrangement between classes, it is quite easy to discern individual topical elements in a number, given sufficient familiarity with Dewey.

In the past several editions, the application of such devices as standard subdivisions (Dewey's Table 1, which lists common concepts applying across subject areas, such as "dictionary," "history," etc.) has been made more consistent across the schedules. With an eye on retrieval and navigation in both OPAC and Web environments, editorial staff have also been standardizing citation order (the order in which topics are combined in notation) and faceting, so that individual components of a Dewey number could form the

Figure 3.4

Dewey Classification Outline

000	Generalities
100	Philosophy & Psychology
200	Religion
300	Social Sciences
400	Language
500	Natural Sciences & Mathematics
600	Technology (Applied Sciences)
700	The Arts; Fine & Decorative Arts
800	Literature & Rhetoric
900	Geography & History

basis for search and retrieval (Mitchell, 1995). As a well-structured scheme available in machine-readable form, Dewey has been adopted by many Internet resource organization projects.

Dewey Examples

CyberDewey

Although not in a library setting, CyberDewey deserves our interest as one of the first Dewey-based Web projects. Mundie (1995) describes how using Dewey enabled him to organize his computer files (as well as everything else in his life, including his medicine cabinet and his son's toys). CyberDewey is Mundie's personal collection of a vast array of Internet resources, each assigned a Dewey number. The opening screen offers a table of the 10 main classes and divisions (with descriptive captions), and one can opt to go directly to each browseable classified list of Internet resources or to browse through captioned section breakdowns (see Figure 3.5). Unannotated resource links are typically assigned four- or five-digit numbers (although some are longer). There is also an alphabetical index of caption text to the sectional level. Incidentally, Mundie makes a strong argument for what he calls ICIP (Internet Cataloguing-in-Publication), and contends that "the right way to organize the Web is with the time-tested tools of library science: MARC, Dewey, LOCSH [*sic*], etc. . . . to do anything else is to re-invent the wheel" (Mundie, 1996).

WWLib—Wolverhampton Web Library

WWLIB is a Web site catalog maintained by the School of Computing and Information Technology at the University of Wolverhampton, England. In addition to direct search by keyword or Dewey number, the classification scheme supports two types of browsing. One shows a scannable shelflist of either the entire catalog or each of the ten main classes. The other is a classification browser, with options to work through hierarchical levels (represented by modified Dewey captions) and leading to portions of the

Figure 3.5

Classification in CyberDewey

A Hotlist of Internet Sites organized using Dewey Decimal Classification codes.

000 Generalities

- 000 Generalities (427)
- 010 Bibliography (60)
- 020 Library and Information Science (47)
- 030 Encyclopedias (14)
- 040 Unassigned (0)
- 050 Magazines (12)
- 060 General organizations and museology (18)
- 070 Journalism (44)
- 080 General collections (9)
- 090 Manuscripts and rare books (0)

500 Science

- 500 Science (50)
- 510 Mathematics (18)
- 520 Astronomy & allied sciences (14)
- 530 Physics (26)
- 540 Chemistry (15)
- 550 Earth sciences (28)
- 560 Paleontology, Paleozoology (10)
- 570 Life sciences (29)
- 580 Botanical sciences (11)
- 590 Zoological Sciences (50)

100 Philosophy and Psychology

- 100 Philosophy (4)
- 110 Metaphysics (2)
- 120 Epistemology, causation, humankind (3)
- 130 Paranormal Phenomena (6)
- 140 Specific philosophical schools (2)
- 150 Psychology (10)
- 160 Logic (4)
- 170 Ethics (2)
- 180 Ancient, mediaeval, Oriental philosophy (0)
- 190 Modern Western philosophy (1)

Dewpoint

Division 020: Library and Information Science

020 Library & information sciences

- 020 CARL
- 020 Faxon
- 020 Foreign Language Cat.
- 020 Information Sciences (WWWVL)
- 020 ISSN Web Page
- 020 Larry's InfoPower
- 020 Library of Congress Web
- 020 Ms. Acquisitions
- 020 U of Chicago
- 020 U of Virginia
- 020 UMI
- 020 University of Strathclyde Department of Information Science

021 Relationships of libraries, archives, information centers

022 Administration of the physical plant

023 Personnel administration

025 Library operations

- 025 eLib: Electronic Libraries Programme (Lycos)
- 025 Internet Public Library (Lycos)

Source: Content extracted from the Dewey Decimal Classification System. Dewey, DDC, and Dewey Decimal Classification are registered trademarks of OCLC Online Computer Library Center, Incorporated. Reprinted with permission.

shelflist for Dewey numbers selected from the browser (see Figure 3.6). The browser expands to as many as six or seven levels, depending on the depth of classification in particular areas.

BUBL Link

The BUBL Information Service, another JISC-funded project, is maintained by the Centre for Digital Library Research at Strathclyde University, Glasgow, Scotland. BUBL services include searchable journal article files, directories, mailing lists, and BUBL Link (Libraries of Networked Knowledge), which is a collection of over 12,000 Internet resource records. Access methods include simple and advanced search, and browse by country, resource type, subject heading (all in one alphabetical list or organized into "subject menus"), and Dewey class. All of these methods interact with each other. For example, country browsing is further subdivided by subject heading when necessary, and subject menu choices may be contextualized by Dewey numbers. Dewey browsing is a simple walk through the scheme (usually not more than four or five levels deep), guided by modified Dewey caption text. Results of searching and browsing are shown as a list of resource titles on the left and metadata records for each resource on the right (see Figure 3.7).

Blue Web'n

Blue Web'n, a project of San Diego State University and Pacific Bell's Education First Initiative, has gathered together an unusual collection of "Internet-based learning applications" (e.g., online tools, information sources, and tutorials). Resources can be searched directly by grade level, application type, content area, Dewey number, and keyword. Users can also browse through a Content Table (a matrix of subject area by resource type) or through the Content Categories, which are based on Dewey but organized into different main classes. Selecting a main category calls up all resources assigned to the entire class; selecting a division restricts retrieval to that division only. Resource links are rated and annotated in accompanying annotations but do not display individual Dewey numbers.

Figure 3.6

Classification in WWLib

WWlib Browse Interface

Use this form to browse the classification listing

Links will expand to matching catalogue extracts. Use the selection buttons and the *examine* button to explore the Dewey Decimal classification hierarchy. This is the 51492nd access since 0925 July 18th.

- ○ 000 Generalities. Catalogues. Newspapers. Computing
- ○ 100 Philosophy. Psychology. The Mind.
- ○ 200 Religion
- ○ 300 Social Sciences. Law. Government. Society. Commerce. Education.
- ○ 400 Linguistics. Scientific Study of Language
- ○ 500 Pure Sciences. Mathematics. Physics. Chemistry. Biology.
- ⊙ 600 Applied Sciences. Engineering. Medicine. Manufacturing.
- ○ 700
- ○ 80
- ○ 90

[Examine]

- ○ 631 Agriculture. Specific Techniques.
- ○ 632 Plant Damage. Plant Injuries. Plant Diseases. Plant Pests. Plant Protection. Vermin.
- ○ 633 Field Crops and their Production
- ○ 634 Horticulture Generally. Orchards. Fruit. Forests.
- ○ 635 Garden Plants. Gardening
- ○ 636 Animal Breeding in General. Breeding of Mammals and Birds. Livestock Rearing. Breeding Of Domestic Animals
- ○ 637 Produce of Domestic Animals and Game
- ○ 638 Keeping, Breeding and Management of Insects and Other Arthropods
- ○ 639 Hunting. Fishing. Fish Breeding

[Examine] [Reset]

- • 631 + University of Aberdeen Department of Agriculture
- • 631 Royal Botanical Gardens Kew

  - o 631.2 Windmills

    - ▪ 631.27 ? Manchester Chestnut Fencing Co.

Source: Content extracted from the Dewey Decimal Classification System. Reprinted with permission.

Figure 3.7

Classification in BUBL Link

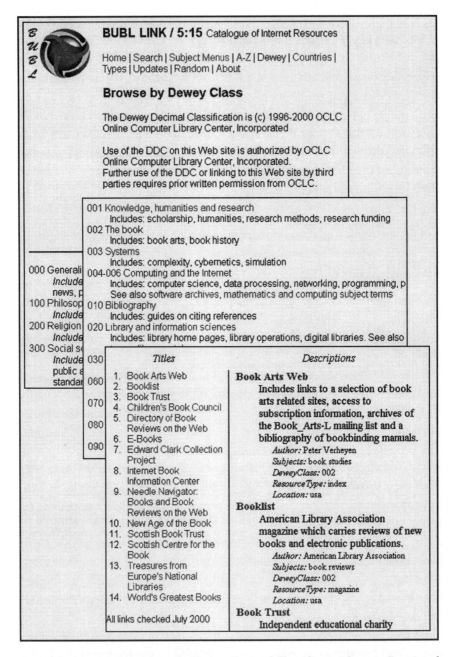

National Library of Canada—Canadian Information by Subject

At the heart of the National Library of Canada's Canadian Information by Subject is a Dewey-arranged shelflist of Internet resources stored on a different page for each main Dewey class. To arrive at these pages, users can browse either an alphabetical list of caption text or the classification in the subject tree, which has a main class list at the top as a navigation tool to reach the division and sections shown underneath. Interestingly, Dewey numbers are expressed in the UDC format rather than classic Dewey (e.g., "4" rather than "400"). In the shelflist, resource links (unannotated, but with augmented titles) are grouped under numbers as detailed as four- and five-digits. Keyword-in-title search is also available.

LCC ON THE WEB

The Library of Congress Classification was developed at the turn of the century, specifically for the Library of Congress collection. Different subject specialists were each responsible for different sections of the classification, which leads to an occasional lack of consistency between sections. Currently LCC is published as 21 classes in over 40 print volumes (the outline is shown in Figure 3.8), with individual indexes and no master index to the entire scheme. New editions appear for individual classes rather than for the scheme as a whole. Between new editions, updates and revisions are published by LC, and these are cumulated for each class by Gale Research. These conditions are expected to change, as the classification has been rendered machine-readable, and several CD-ROM products have appeared. Full LCC numbers are assigned to all USMARC records created by LC catalogers, thereby reducing cataloging effort (and cost) for libraries which choose to use LCC. This is one of the reasons that so many academic libraries use LCC, another being that the classification scheme was designed to meet the organizing needs of a large research collection.

LCC is hierarchical in arrangement and is very much an enumerative classification scheme. The notation is alphanumeric—LCC

Figure 3.8

LC Classification Outline

A	General Works
B	Philosophy, Psychology, Religion
C	Auxiliary Sciences of History
D	History: General and Old World
E	History: America
F	History: America
G	Geography, Anthropology, Recreation
H	Social Sciences
J	Political Science
K	Law
L	Education
M	Music and Books on Music
N	Fine Arts
P	Language and Literature
Q	Science
R	Medicine
S	Agriculture
T	Technology
U	Military Science
V	Naval Science
Z	Library Science

subject numbers consist of one or more letters representing main class and subclass (usually discipline-based), followed by a number between 1 and 9999 (including decimal numbers) representing divisions, subdivisions, and narrower aspects of a subject. In many cases specific topics or geographic place names are further specified by Cutter numbers (letter and number combinations). Some examples of topics and their numbers can be seen in Figure 3.9. Although LCC does make use of tables for building numbers, these are specific to individual classes and subclasses and are applied in more restrictive circumstances than is the case with Dewey. LCC does not lend itself quite so well to hyperlinked browsing as Dewey and is found less often as a navigational device on the Internet.

LCC Examples

CyberStacks(sm)

CyberStacks(sm) was developed by Gerry McKiernan at Iowa State University Library. Research and scholarly Internet resources in the sciences (including monographs, serials, files, and search services) are assigned one or more abridged LC numbers. Users can browse from broad class letter to subclass letters (with topical icons) to division number ranges, and then to resources with abridged LC numbers, rich extracts, and summaries (see Figure 3.10). The site also contains an alphabetical title list of resources and a cross-classification index by LCC caption text.

Scout Report Signpost

A National Science Foundation (NSF)–funded project at the University of Wisconsin–Madison, Signpost provides access to upwards of 9,000 Internet resources. The opening page presents options for full-text search, fielded search (for cataloged items, about half of the collection), and browse by Library of Congress subject heading (this part is discussed more fully in Chapter 4) and by LCC. The classification scheme is displayed as a table of broad headings, with LC class letters underneath. Browsing this list proceeds to ar-

Figure 3.9

Examples of LC Classification Numbers

HF5549.5.A4   Alcoholism in the workplace
  H   Social sciences
    HF   Commerce
      5000–   Business
        5549   Personnel management
          5549.5   Special topics, A–Z
            A4   Alcoholism

HV864.A2   Residential child care in Alabama
  H   Social sciences
    HV   Social pathology; Social and public welfare;
                  Criminology
      697–   Protection, assistance, and relief
                    Special classes
        701–   Children
          862–   Residential care
            863–   United States
              864   By region or state, A–Z
                A2   Alabama

Figure 3.10

Classification in CyberStacks(sm)

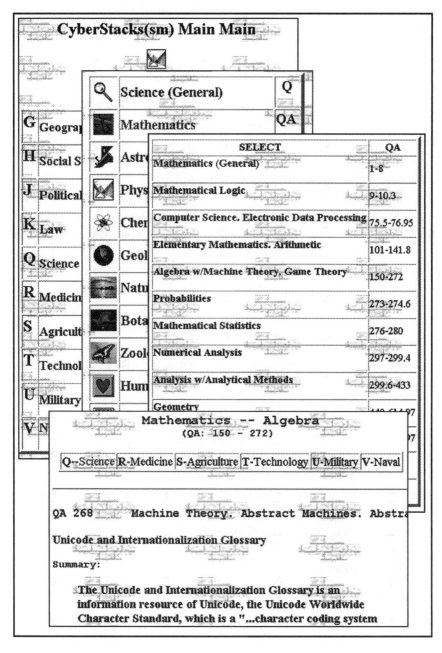

Reprinted with permission.

rays of captioned class/subclass letters, and then to item listings. Signpost records (based on the Dublin Core) include substantial annotations, general cataloging information, rich subject indexing, and one or more LC numbers (see Figure 3.11).

UDC ON THE WEB

The Universal Decimal Classification is an adaptation of Dewey, developed under the auspices of the Fédération internationale du documentation (FID), and now maintained in The Hague by a consortium of publishers. Full, medium, and abridged editions, and individual subject sections, have been appearing since the early 1900s in over 20 languages. The English medium edition forms the basis for the machine-readable UDC Master Reference File. While the initial intent was to use UDC for subject access as part of an ambitious universal bibliography project, the scheme was widely adopted by European libraries and is also used by some secondary services. UDC retains Dewey's general arrangement of classes and divisions, and a version of the Dewey notation, but differs dramatically in the area of number building. UDC applies the principles of facet analysis more liberally, allowing for concatenation of complete notational strings and for wider application of common and special auxiliary tables.

Future plans for UDC include the creation of a totally faceted scheme (McIlwaine, 1995b, 1998). Recently, the UDC Consortium entered into an arrangement with the Bliss Classification Association to work more closely together in developing new classes and schedules (the Bliss Classification is one the few large general schemes which is fully faceted, but it is not yet used widely, and not at all on the Web to this point). The editors of UDC and DDC are also moving toward greater cooperation and standardization.

UDC Examples

NISS—Directory of Networked Resources

NISS (National Information Services and Systems in the United Kingdom) maintains a database of Internet resources classified by

Figure 3.11

Classification in Scout Report Signpost

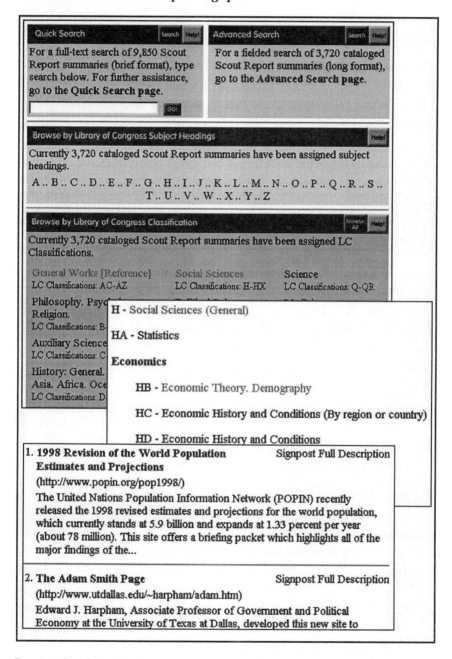

Reprinted with permission.

subject experts, using UDC. The NISS Directory opens with a hundreds breakdown, and proceeds through hierarchical levels, showing resource descriptions (with annotations) classified at each level. Resource descriptions include title, owner, resource type, contact details, copyright information, keywords, UDC numbers, and a description (see Figure 3.12). Users can also browse by alphabetical topic (seemingly a chain index to the UDC) and shelf order, and search by title, UDC number, or words appearing in any record field.

GERHARD—German Harvest Automated Retrieval and Directory

GERHARD uses UDC by mapping natural language verbalizations (in German, English, and French) onto 70,000 UDC hierarchies to provide browsing through over a million harvested Web pages. Each item is assigned one or more UDC numbers (never seen by the user). GERHARD accommodates simple and advanced (field-based) searching through resources, as well as keyword search through the UDC-based directory. Browsing through the directory displays (in text) the hierarchical path, the number of items, the number of items classified at each displayed level, and the number of items in the entire tree subordinate to each displayed level.

OTHER LIBRARY CLASSIFICATION SCHEMES

American Mathematical Society (AMS)— Mathematics on the Web

The AMS' Mathematics on the Web site provides a tabular view of an Internet resource pathfinder, as well as terse and verbose text versions. Buried in the contents are two interesting pages which gather Internet resource titles: "Materials Organized by Mathematical Subject Classification" and "Materials Organized by Mathematical Topics." The former (about 60 class numbers from the 1991 edition of the AMS Classification) is based on a list by D.R. Wilkins at Trinity College, Dublin, and the latter (some 40 categories) on a page at the University of Tennessee, Knoxville.

Figure 3.12

Classification in NISS

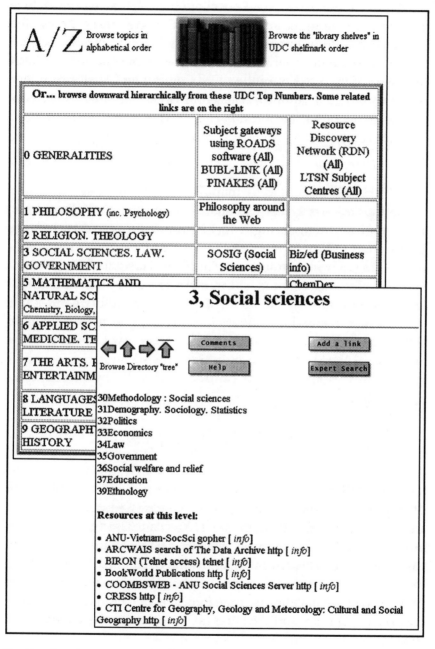

A/Z Browse topics in alphabetical order

Browse the "library shelves" in UDC shelfmark order

Or... browse downward hierarchically from these UDC Top Numbers. Some related links are on the right

	Subject gateways using ROADS software (All) BUBL-LINK (All) PINAKES (All)	Resource Discovery Network (RDN) (All) LTSN Subject Centres (All)
0 GENERALITIES		
1 PHILOSOPHY (inc. Psychology)	Philosophy around the Web	
2 RELIGION. THEOLOGY		
3 SOCIAL SCIENCES. LAW. GOVERNMENT	SOSIG (Social Sciences)	Biz/ed (Business info)
5 MATHEMATICS AND NATURAL SCI... Chemistry, Biology,		ChemDex
6 APPLIED SC... MEDICINE. TE...		
7 THE ARTS. ... ENTERTAINM...		
8 LANGUAGES LITERATURE		
9 GEOGRAPH... HISTORY		

3, Social sciences

Browse Directory "tree"

[Comments] [Add a link]
[Help] [Expert Search]

30 Methodology : Social sciences
31 Demography. Sociology. Statistics
32 Politics
33 Economics
34 Law
35 Government
36 Social welfare and relief
37 Education
39 Ethnology

Resources at this level:

- ANU-Vietnam-SocSci gopher [info]
- ARCWAIS search of The Data Archive http [info]
- BIRON (Telnet access) telnet [info]
- BookWorld Publications http [info]
- COOMBSWEB - ANU Social Sciences Server http [info]
- CRESS http [info]
- CTI Centre for Geography, Geology and Meteorology: Cultural and Social Geography http [info]

Reprinted with permission of NISS (a division of EduServ).

Association for Computing Machinery (ACM)—CoRR

The Computing Research Repository (CoRR) is an e-print archive sponsored by the Association for Computing Machinery (ACM), the Los Alamos e-Print archive, and the Networked Computer Science Technical Reference Library (NCSTRL). Papers collected in CoRR are classified by codes from the ACM Computing Classification System, and also by a list of constructed broad subject areas (which are cross-listed to ACM classification codes). The subject areas are used to browse the collection, and ACM codes can be used in searching.

Engineering Index (Ei)—EELS and EEVL

Both of these engineering collections employ the Ei Thesaurus, developed by Engineering Information, Inc. (now a part of the Elsevier family), publishers of *Engineering Index* and many other engineering information services. The Ei Thesaurus includes descriptors and classification codes, the hierarchical component. In the Engineering E-Library, Sweden (EELS), developed by the Swedish University of Technology Libraries, each cataloged item is assigned both descriptors and classification codes. Users can browse through hierarchical layers of the classification scheme and scan resources indexed to various levels, or can search directly by classification number, title, descriptor, description, and URL. Searches can also be limited by general class number (see Figure 3.13).

The Edinburgh Engineering Virtual Library (EEVL) is funded under the eLib program and is hosted at Heriot-Watt University Library in Edinburgh, Scotland. EEVL's search function, EASIER, retrieves information from three collections: the EEVL Catalog of descriptive metadata, an archive of engineering newsgroup postings, and the full text of all cataloged U.K. sites. The Catalog can be browsed by categories and subcategories using an in-house system based on the Ei Thesaurus. EEVL is one of the first "hubs" of the RDN gateway directory service, and cooperates with EELS, the Australasian Virtual Engineering Library (AVEL), Scout Report Signpost in the United States, and Elsevier Engineering Information's Ei Village.

Figure 3.13

Classification in EELS

1. Browse EELS
   Browse engineering resources classified using Engineering Information, Inc.'s
   EI classification.
   - o 400 Civil Engineering
   - o 500 Mining Engineering
   - o 600 Mechanical Engineering
   - o 700 Electrical Engineering

700 Electrical Engineering

- 700 Electrical Engineering, General
- 710 Electronics and Communication Engineering
- 720 Computers and Data Processing
- 730 Control Engineering
- 740 Light and Optical Technology
- 750 Sound and Acoustical Technology

All fields (below) ▼		Ei 700 and below ▼

All fields (below)
Title
URL
Description
Subject
Ei Classification

| Browse | Search | Comments | Help

- 700 Electrical Engineering
  - o **720 Computers and Data Processing** ◄
    - 721 Computer Circuits and Logic Elements
    - 722 Computer Hardware
    - 723 Computer Software, Data Handling and Applications

All fields (below) ▼		Ei 720 and below ▼

Future Generation Computer Systems
   DE: Computer science
   Home page for Future Generation Computer Systems published by Elsevier
   Science.

National Agricultural Library (NAL)—AgDB

AgDB, the Agriculture-Related Information Systems, Databases, and Datasets, is a project contributed to the Agriculture Network Information Center (AgNIC) by the U.S. National Agricultural Library. Records are listed alphabetically by resource name or can be searched by keyword or AGRICOLA category code. The AGRICOLA category codes (used in the database of the same name) can be browsed in hierarchical order or in alphabetical order by code name.

U.S. National Library of Medicine (NLM)—OMNI

OMNI (Organising Medical Networked Information) is co-sponsored by the U.K. National Institute for Medical Research, in association with a number of similar institutions, and uses ROADS software. Users can get to resource listings by browsing a systematic list of NLM classification codes, an alphabetical list of code names, or an alphabetical list of terms from NLM's Medical Subject Headings (MeSH). Classification browsing presents an array of numbers or terms, selection from which leads to resource titles which are linked to short descriptive records, including a field of linked keywords, allowing for search expansion. OMNI's application of MeSH is illustrated in Chapter 4.

PURPOSE-SPECIFIC CLASSIFICATION SCHEMES

There may not always be an appropriate scheme for a particular collection, or the expertise to apply the scheme may be lacking. In the absence of a library classification, many Web sites offer resource links organized by type or by a list of subject categories created for the purpose. These ad hoc alphabetical (and sometimes numeric) arrangements are often the work of one or more individuals and tend to disintegrate when the individual is no longer involved. Most search services also provide collections of reviewed or partner material in categories. Yahoo is probably the best-known and the best-developed example (Dodd, 1996), but there are many others developed for specific subject areas or specialized collections.

The WWW Virtual Library (WWWVL)

The WWWVL Project was started at CERN (the European Lab for Particle Physics), the birthplace of the Web. These days the WWWVL is regarded as one of many search services, but when the Web was a new phenomenon this was the common starting point for finding resource links arranged in a browseable order. The screen opens with a main class list, browseable one level further, and from there to a page of resource links maintained by one or another participating institution or individual, the idea being to create and maintain a distributed virtual library of evaluated and annotated resources. Whether maintained at the project site or at a participating institution, a seamless look is created for all pages by the consistent layout and the use of the WWWVL logo.

THE FUTURE OF CLASSIFICATION

The unbounded growth of Internet resources has given new prominence to the role of library classifications in imposing order on chaos. The impact of this new application area on the study of classification can be seen in journals such as *Knowledge Organization*, the *Journal of Internet Cataloging*, and *Cataloging and Classification Quarterly*, and at meetings of groups such as the International Society for Knowledge Organization (ISKO) and the Special Interest Group on Classification Research (SIG CR) of the American Society for Information Science (ASIS).

Within and outside of the field of classification research, there is general agreement that classification is desirable in helping users cope with complex resource collections. Any individual or institution seeking to organize a large body of Internet resources is likely to present lists and links arranged in some categorized fashion—hence the increasingly common adoption of the Yahoo model in the realm of intranets (Nielsen, 1998; Rosenfeld, 1998), and the call for "taxonomists" in the realm of knowledge management.

Classification schemes offer a number of advantages (Chan, 1995; Koch, 1997; Koh, 1995; McKiernan, 1997):

- They afford browsing and navigation, which is especially useful in unfamiliar subject areas;
- Query terms can be contextualized within the hierarchical structure of the scheme;
- Search results can be filtered through limiting to classes and categories;
- Hierarchies can be used to broaden and narrow a search;
- A large group of items can be partitioned into smaller groups;
- Classes and categories can be employed in the creation of user profiles;
- "Shelflists" can be used to analyze collections of virtual resources, just as they are used to assess physical library collections;
- Classification, as structure rather than language, suggests possibilities for multilingual access; and
- Classification schemes have the potential for acting as switching devices between different subject languages.

Existing library classifications have the added advantages of institutionalization (an ongoing agency is responsible for maintenance and updating), familiarity to users and staff, and availability in machine-readable form.

In contrast, home-grown schemes, even those with well-developed terminological policies such as Yahoo (Callery & Tracy-Proulx, 1997), suffer from a lack of understanding of the principles of classification design and development. The larger the collection grows, the more confusing and overwhelming a poorly designed hierarchy becomes (Koch, 1997; Nielsen, 1998; Rosenfeld, 1998). Dodd (1996) and Vizine-Goetz (1996b) have both compared Yahoo to traditional library classifications, and found that while the structures can be mapped to some degree, the terminology and arrangement of categories (especially with respect to main classes) tend to differ.

Classification researchers are identifying some of the problems encountered in using library classification schemes for networked resources. Current library classification schemes are primarily based on academic disciplines, which may not be appropriate for the interdisciplinary and multidisciplinary environment of the Internet, and which also may not concur with the personalized knowledge structures of users. Considering this and other disadvantages of current schemes, some suggest that new types of classification schemes and new ways of thinking about classification may be needed (Beghtol, 1998; Dahlberg, 1995; Hjørland & Albrechtsen, 1998; Williamson, 1997). Beghtol in particular looks at the impact on classification of expected changes in scholarly communication:

> The next century of classification theory, practice, and research will need to react rapidly to multidisciplinary literary warrant and to build responsiveness to different discourse communities into the concept of consensus. In order to promote intellectual exchange, research, and education that, in the electronic environment, are not limited by time, place, or a static discourse community, basic research is needed on structural principles and creative design criteria for classification systems. (Beghtol, 1998, p. 8)

Be that as it may, there are undeniable advantages to using existing library classifications and, in many cases, steps are being taken to make traditional schemes more amenable to a networked environment. The following points have been identified as desiderata for a classification scheme intended for networked resources (Beghtol, 1998; Dahlberg, 1995; Koh, 1995; Molholt, 1995; Vizine-Goetz, 1996a, 1996b):

- Currency, hospitality for new topics, and capability for accommodating new terminology;
- Flexibility and expandability—including possibilities for decomposing faceted notation for retrieval purposes;
- Intelligibility, intuitiveness, and transparency—it should be easy for the user to use, responsive to individual learning styles, able to adjust to the interests of users, and allow for custom views;

- Universality—the scheme should be applicable for different types of collections and communities and should be able to be integrated with other subject languages; and

- Authoritativeness—there should be a method of reaching consensus on terminology, structure, revision, and so on, but that consensus should include user communities.

Editors and staff responsible for the major classification schemes are responding to these needs. Cooperative efforts among UDC, Dewey, and the Bliss Classification were mentioned earlier. UDC, Dewey, and LCC are all being examined for ways to increase the identification of facets in notation and to incorporate terminology from schedule captions and text. Having a scheme in a machine-readable database provides an opportunity to incorporate superordinate hierarchical information for topics at all levels, which is especially useful in the case of LCC, where the notation is not expressive (i.e., does not reflect hierarchies). Broadbent (1995) speaks of this advantage, and also describes the development of alphabetical indexes to the classification using several different methods.

Researchers working with Dewey at OCLC have shown themselves to be especially cognizant of the potential role of classification in the digital era. The work of Vizine-Goetz and colleagues at OCLC and in partnership with NetLab at Lund University, Sweden, includes testing Dewey as a method for automatic text description enrichment, examining different navigational interfaces, mapping LCSH to Dewey numbers, automating Dewey number assignment, and identifying high-use class numbers for transformation into more popular terminology (Koch & Vizine-Goetz, 1999; Thompson, Shafer, & Vizine-Goetz, 1997; Vizine-Goetz, 1996a, 1996b, 1998).

Such research in the application of library classification to Internet resources should lead to modifications to traditional schemes to make them more amenable to this new environment. This in turn may lead to wider adoption of these formal and well-maintained structures. Alternatively, as suggested by Albrechtsen and Jacob (1998), among others, the transformation of classification from "a tool for establishment of order and control over the collection to a boundary object functioning to create cohesion across diverse information ecologies" (p. 310) may be realized by collaboration between classificationists and user communities.

REFERENCES

Albrechtsen, Hanne, & Jacob, Elin K. (1998). The dynamics of classification systems as boundary objects for cooperation in the electronic library. *Library Trends, 47,* 293–312.

Beghtol, Clare. (1998). Knowledge domains: Multidisciplinarity and bibliographic classification systems. *Knowledge Organization, 25*(1/2), 1–12.

A brief introduction to the Dewey Decimal Classification. (1998, September 12). Retrieved January 5, 1999 from the World Wide Web: http://www.oclc.org/oclc/fp/about/brief.htm.

Broadbent, Elaine. (1995). Classification access in the online catalog. *Cataloging & Classification Quarterly, 21*(2), 119–142.

Callery, Anne, & Tracy-Proulx, Deb. (1997). Yahoo! Cataloging the Web. *Journal of Internet Cataloging, 1*(1), 57–64.

Carpenter, Michael, & Svenonius, Elaine. (1985). *Foundations of cataloging: A sourcebook.* Englewood, CO: Libraries Unlimited.

Chan, Lois Mai. (1994). *Cataloguing and classification: An introduction* (2nd ed.). New York: McGraw-Hill.

Chan, Lois Mai. (1995). Classification, present and future. *Cataloging & Classification Quarterly, 21*(2), 5–18.

Chan, Lois Mai. (1999). *A guide to the Library of Congress classification* (5th ed.). Englewood, CO: Libraries Unlimited.

Chan, Lois Mai, Comaromi, John P., Mitchell, Joan S., & Satija, Mohinder P. (1996). *Dewey decimal classification: A practical guide* (2nd ed., rev. for DDC21). Albany, NY: Forest Press.

Dahlberg, Ingetraut. (1995). The future of classification in libraries and networks: A theoretical point of view. *Cataloging & Classification Quarterly, 21*(2), 23–36.

Daniel, Ruth, & Mills, J. (1975). *A classification of library & information science.* London: Library Association.

Dodd, David G. (1996). Grass-roots cataloging and classification: Food for thought from World Wide Web subject-oriented hierarchical lists. *Library Resources & Technical Services, 40,* 275–286.

Hjørland, Birger, & Albrechtsen, Hanne. (1998). *An analysis of some trends in classification research.* Paper distributed at ASIS '98: Information access in the global information economy, October 24–29, 1998, Pittsburgh, PA.

Koch, Traugott. (1997, February 28). *The role of classification schemes in Internet resource description and discovery* (DESIRE project deliverable: Specification for resource description methods, Part 3). Retrieved November 27, 1998 from the World Wide Web: http://www.ub2.lu.se/desire/radar/reports/D3.2.3/class_v10.html.

Koch, Traugott, & Vizine-Goetz, Diane. (1999, June 16). *Automatic classification and content navigation support for Web services: DESIRE II cooperates with OCLC.* Retrieved January 4, 2000 from the World Wide Web: http://www.oclc.org/oclc/research/publications/review98/koch_vizine-goetz/automatic.htm.

Koh, Gertrude S. (1995). Options in classification available through modern technology. *Cataloging & Classification Quarterly, 19*(3/4), 195–211.

Kwasnik, Barbara. (1999). The role of classification in knowledge representation and discovery. *Library Trends, 48,* 22–47.

McIlwaine, Ia. (1998). UDC: Into the 21st century. *Aslib Proceedings, 50*(2), 44–48.

McIlwaine, Ia C. (1995a). *Guide to the use of UDC* (rev. ed.). The Hague, Netherlands: IFLA.

McIlwaine, Ia C. (1995b). UCD centenary: The present state and future prospects. *Knowledge Organisation, 22,* 64–69.

McKiernan, Gerry. (1997). The new/old World Wide Web order: The application of "neo-conventional" functionality to facilitate access and use of a WWW database of science and technology resources. *Journal of Internet Cataloging, 1*(1), 47–55.

Mitchell, Joan S. (1995). DDC 21 and beyond: The Dewey Decimal Classification prepares for the future. *Cataloging & Classification Quarterly, 21*(2), 37–47.

Molholt, Pat. (1995). Qualities of classification schemes for the information superhighway. *Cataloging & Classification Quarterly, 21*(2), 19–22.

Mundie, David A. (1995, November 12). *Organizing computer resources.* Retrieved January 5, 1999 from the World Wide Web: http://ivory.lm.com/~mundie/DDHC/organizing_computers.html.

Mundie, David A. (1996, April 18). *Internet cataloguing-in-publication.* Retrieved January 5, 1999 from the World Wide Web: http://ivory.lm.com/~mundie/CyberDewey/ICIP.html.

Nielsen, Jakob. (1998, November 1). Why Yahoo is good (but may get worse).

Jakob Nielsen's Alertbox. Retrieved January 7, 1999 from the World Wide Web: http://www.useit.com/alertbox/981101.html.

Painter, Ann F. (Ed.). (1972). *Reader in classification and descriptive cataloging*. Washington, DC: NCR Microcard Editions.

Rosenfeld, Lou. (1998, December 4). Yahoo! is dead. Long live Yahoo!: An obligatory Yahoo! rant. *Web Review*. Retrieved January 7, 1999 from the World Wide Web: http://webreview.com/wr/pub/98/12/04/arch/index.html.

Taylor, Arlene G. (1999). *The organization of information*. Englewood, CO: Libraries Unlimited.

Taylor, Arlene G. (2000). *Wynar's introduction to cataloging and classification* (9th ed.). Englewood, CO: Libraries Unlimited.

Thompson, Roger, Shafer, Keith, & Vizine-Goetz, Diane. (1997). Evaluating Dewey concepts as a knowledge base for automatic subject assignment. In R.B. Allen & E. Rasmussen (Eds.), *ACM Digital Libraries '97: Proceedings of the 2nd ACM International Conference on Digital Libraries* (pp. 37–46). New York: ACM.

Vizine-Goetz, Diane. (1996a). Online classification; Implications for classifying and document[-like object] retrieval. In R. Green (Ed.), *Knowledge organization and change: Proceedings of the fourth international ISKO Conference, 15–18 July 1996, Washington, DC, USA* (pp. 249–253). Fankfurt/Main, Germany: Indeks Verlag.

Vizine-Goetz, Diane. (1996b, January 19). *Using library classification schemes for Internet resources* (OCLC Internet Cataloging Project Colloquium position paper). Retrieved January 5, 1999 from the World Wide Web: http://www.oclc.org/oclc/man/colloq/v-g.htm.

Vizine-Goetz, Diane. (1998). OCLC investigates using classification tools to organize Internet data. In P.A. Cochrane & E.H. Johnson (Eds.), *Visualizing subject access for 21st century information resources* (pp. 93–105). Champaign, IL: Graduate School of Library and Information Science, University of Illinois at Urbana–Champaign (Clinic on Library Applications of Data Processing, 1997).

Williamson, Nancy J. (1997). Classification in the millennium. *Online & CD-ROM Review, 21*, 298–301.

WEB PAGE

Classification on the 'Net. http://www.simmons.edu/~schwartz/myclass.html.

4

Controlled
Vocabularies

In most bibliographic retrieval systems (e.g., library catalogs, online databases, or metadata projects), a considerable amount of time and effort is spent on assigning alphabetical subject terms to records in order to enhance retrieval. These terms generally come from a prescribed indexing language of some kind. Although a classification scheme is also an indexing language, the focus here is on alphabetical subject indexing languages, variously called controlled vocabularies, thesauri, subject headings lists, descriptor lists, term lists, and keyword lists (the names are not used with any consistency, although each carries certain connotations). Many such tools derive from a long history of development in the context of libraries and indexing and abstracting services. This chapter will examine different types of alphabetical subject analysis systems which are being applied to the organization of networked resources.

BACKGROUND

While subject access of one form or another has been a feature of libraries and information services since their inception, our understanding of controlled vocabularies and the role they play in information retrieval has been primarily advanced by formal studies which began with Cutter's *Rules for a Dictionary Catalog* in 1876 (Cutter, 1904) and continue through Metcalfe's (1957) writings on alphabetico-specific indexing; Coates' (1960) theories on subject analysis, applied to the *British Technology Index*; Ranganathan's seminal studies of facet analysis (Ranganathan, 1967); and Austin's work on PRECIS (Austin, 1974). Chan, Richmond, and Svenonius' (1985) collection of key readings in subject analysis includes works by some of these authors, as well as many other pioneers. Texts by Foskett (1996) and Lancaster (1972, 1986, 1998) provide thorough reviews of both intellectually developed and automatic approaches to indexing and retrieval. Insights into subject indexing practices in cataloging can be found in Chan's (1995) frequently updated analysis of the structure and application of Library of Congress subject headings (LCSH), as well as in introductory cataloging textbooks (Chan, 1994; A.G. Taylor, 1999, 2000).

Why Controlled Vocabulary?

In the context of a world of machine-readable text, one might be surprised to learn that the application of intellectually developed subject indexing tools is still a common practice. Certainly there has been significant progress in retrieval from machine-readable text using statistical, and to some degree linguistic, characteristics. Search engines in particular have brought this kind of processing to the general end user, as discussed in Chapter 5, although it is important to note that research into automatic text processing for information retrieval goes back to the 1950s (see Stevens, Giuliano, & Heilprin, 1965) and has most recently been advanced thanks to the activities of the Association for Computing Machinery's Special Interest Group for Information Retrieval (ACM SIGIR), and the annual Text REtrieval Conference (TREC), discussed in more detail in Chapter 6.

To take one obvious application for controlled vocabulary, in cases where databases do not contain full text, subject description augments what little information may be available for searching (the MARC record in a library catalog being a good example). The need for textual access points of some kind is also evident where surrogates in a database represent non-text objects (e.g., images and sound). Techniques for pattern matching in image and sound retrieval, or in automatic indexing and abstracting of video, while fascinating, are still largely in research and development.

Even in settings where an abundance of text is available for searching, there is still a case to be made for applying controlled vocabularies. The sources of so-called "free" or "natural language" text for searching can range from titles to abstracts to full text. Depending on the length of the document, free text can add many access points to the indexing of an item. This tends to have benefits for recall (a measure of the degree to which all relevant items in a file are retrieved in response to a query), since the access is that much richer. Free text also has the advantage of offering more specific terminology than is usually found in controlled vocabularies, and more current terminology, since the editorial process of revising a controlled vocabulary can be time-consuming. However, free text can also lead to failures in precision (a measure of the proportion of relevant items in a set of retrieved results), since the longer the text representation, the more chance there is that some of the text will refer to concepts which are not central to the theme of the document. Rich free text can also be a source of false drops, where the intended relationship between several terms used by a searcher may retrieve documents in which those terms are in a different relationship or are not related to each other at all.

In a very large file (Internet search engine collections being an extreme example), a topic of interest may have been expressed in diverse ways in text, and the burden is on the searcher to imagine what these might be. Despite redundancy in natural language expression, the greater the diversity, the greater the likelihood that recall will suffer, whether the system at hand is a ranking algorithm or an interface offering tools such as Boolean operators, proximity statements, and the like. Controlled vocabulary reduces the effort of accounting for synonymous expressions and can further provide additional search terms through exploiting structured interterm relationships. On the other hand, human indexers, being human, may make errors in indexing, and indexing languages provide their own constraints on the ability of indexers to achieve sufficient exhaustivity (breadth of topical coverage when indexing an item) and specificity (depth of topical expression).

There is no denying that controlled vocabularies are costly to create and apply, and that they can be difficult for end users to use directly. Over the past 40 years, researchers have tested (and scholars have debated about) the merits of using controlled vocabularies. These research efforts and the issue they raise are well reviewed by Lancaster (1998, ch. 14) and Rowley (1994), and Soergel (1994) offers a cogent examination of the effects of indexing devices on retrieval performance. Findings have varied, but the general consensus, if one can be said to exist, is that each plays an important role and is useful for different types of retrieval objectives and settings.

As use of large online systems has moved from the search intermediary to the end user, some researchers have called for a focus on thesauri for searchers rather than (or in addition to) indexers (see, for example, Anderson & Rowley, 1992; Bates, 1989; Cochrane, 1992; Schatz, Johnson, & Cochrane, 1996). Aitchison, Gilchrist, and Bawden (1997) lay out a typology which includes thesauri used in both indexing and searching (the classic model); thesauri used for indexing only, where the end user relies on free text and the thesaurus serves to augment queries with additional terminology; and thesauri used in searching only, where the purpose of the thesaurus is to suggest terminology for free text query expansion.

Controlled Vocabulary Components

Although many indexing languages, especially older ones, were built on an ad hoc basis, there are standards and guidelines governing thesaurus construction (International Organization for Standardization, 1986; National Information Standards Organization, 1994) and index content, organization, and presentation (Anderson, 1997; International Organization for Standardization, 1996). A very thorough review of the theory and practice of vocabulary development is found in Soergel (1974), and the invaluable practical manual by

Aitchison, Gilchrist, and Bawden (1997) is the best source for advice on building and maintaining effective thesauri.

The components of an indexing language include:

Vocabulary

- "Preferred" terms (words or phrases) applied in indexing—descriptors, subject headings, keywords, and so on (in classification, the notation); and
- "Non-preferred" terms not used in indexing, but which lead to preferred terms (e.g., "Periodicals, use Serials").

Syntactic and Semantic Elements

- Grammar governing the construction of a subject string (e.g., "Libraries—Canada—History");
- During the vocabulary construction phase, policies regarding the inclusion of preferred terms which combine concepts (e.g., "School Libraries"); and
- Semantic connections among preferred terms—hierarchical and other types of relationships (e.g., "Academic Libraries, narrower term College Libraries").

Display

- Mechanism(s) through which elements of the indexing language are shown to indexers or end users, whether on a printed page or a computer screen.

Application Policies

- Policies regarding such things as indexing exhaustivity and specificity; minimum and maximum number of terms; assignment of roles, links, or weights; and so on.

Management

- Systems through which the indexing language is maintained, revised, and managed.

These elements are present to a greater or lesser degree depending on the sophistication of the indexing language, and also on its intended use.

Precoordinate and Postcoordinate Indexing

The distinction between precoordinate and postcoordinate indexing has to do with how indexing systems represent the multiplicity of topics manifested in the content of an object. Beyond a broad categorical naming (e.g., "transportation"), an object may discuss several different topics (e.g., "railroads," "automobiles," "airlines," and "interstate bus systems"), aspects of a topic (e.g., "economics" as opposed to "history"), location (e.g., "in the United States"), and so on. In a precoordinate indexing system, the indexer attempts to characterize content by creating one or more subject strings which bring preferred terms together and imply roles and relationships among them (e.g., "Railroads—Economic aspects— United States—Bibliography"). These strings are constrained by the grammar and policies of the indexing language. In postcoordinate indexing, content characterization is achieved through the assignment of individual preferred terms (again, subject to indexing policies in place), without an attempt to bring those terms together into a relationship. Concept coordination is left to the point where the searcher creates a query which specifies a relationship and which often does not rely on any knowledge of the controlled vocabulary. The query might take advantage of available search commands such as Boolean operators, truncation, and proximity statements (e.g., "select (railroad? or railway?) and (economic? or financ?) and (united states or u(w)s)"), or might be as simple as "railroad economics in the U.S." Figure 4.1 illustrates these two approaches.

Traditionally, precoordinate indexing is used in print-based systems (such as card catalogs and print indexing services) and postcoordinate systems in machine-readable database settings (e.g., commercial online databases). Precoordinate systems offer some advantages, even in an online setting. Every word or phrase in a precoordinate heading is contextualized by the other parts of the heading—this can be useful in searching and also in results display. For purposes of browsing, fewer items will be gathered together under each precoordinate heading than would be the case in a postcoordinate indexing application. A weakness of most precoordinate systems is that the characterization of subject content

Figure 4.1

Precoordinate and Postcoordinate Indexing

Understanding the Business of Library Acquisitions (Karen A. Schmidt, 1999)	
Precoordinate Indexing (Library of Congress Subject Headings)	**Postcoordinate Indexing** (Thesaurus of ERIC Descriptors)
Acquisitions (Libraries)—United States	Ethics Information Industry * Library Acquisition * Library Administration * Library Collection Development * Library Material Selection Library Personnel Media Selection Nonprint Media Printed Materials Publishing Industry Scholarly Journals Vendors [* indicates a major descriptor]

tends to be broad, and indexing is often limited to a small number of subject strings. Another problem concerns the difficulty of conveying the correct combination order to users: Is it "Railroads—Economic aspects—United States," or "United States—Economic aspects—Railroads"? This problem is overcome to some degree in online environments, where precoordinate subject headings can be indexed for individual words and subunits as well as entire strings, and can be displayed in several different orderings.

The application of postcoordinate indexing usually results in a richer number of controlled language access points, although this richness can bring along the problems of precision failure and false drops mentioned earlier. Some of these problems can be overcome by assigning weights to terms which are central to the theme of an item or by assigning roles which indicate the relationship among terms. It is difficult to use postcoordinate indexing as a browsing mechanism, however, since each term may index a large number of items and contextual information is lacking.

Both precoordinate and postcoordinate applications have been applied to collections of networked resources. The following section describes a sampling of the use of controlled vocabularies for subject access. Applications run the gamut from using subject descriptors for organizing collections of URLs to exhaustive indexing of object surrogates in databases.

CONTROLLED VOCABULARY APPLICATIONS

Library of Congress Subject Headings

The Library of Congress Subject Headings (LCSH), first published in 1914 and reaching its twenty-third edition in 2000, is the precoordinate vocabulary used by LC catalogers for subject access to all cataloged materials. It has become the standard subject access tool for large (and many small) libraries in the English-speaking world, and has been translated into several languages. LCSH is published in print (in five volumes), on microfiche, and on CD-ROM as part of *Classification Plus*, and the subject authority file is available for search in bibliographic utilities such as OCLC. Catalogers using LCSH generally attempt to replicate policy and practice at LC, which was not widely shared in any detail until the publication of Chan's text (now in its third edition, 1995), and several manuals from the LC Cataloging Distribution Service (Chan, 1990; Library of Congress, Cataloging Policy and Support Office, 1996).

Subject headings consist of a main heading, which may stand alone but is more normally followed by one or more subdivisions. Subdivisions can be topical, chronological, geographic, or identifying form (see examples of LC subject headings in Figure 4.2). Although LC policy allows up to 10 subject headings to be assigned to one item, current practice usually results in from one to four. Assigned headings are supposed to be specific and coextensive with the item—for example, if the topic is the anatomy of Siamese cats, then the main heading should be "Siamese cat—Anatomy," not "Cats—Anatomy," and not "Anatomy." This general rule is overridden for several categories of subject (e.g., biography) and is not possible when specific concepts are not represented by authorized headings.

LCSH is used for subject access in cases where metadata projects take a classic cataloging approach, and also appears in a number of resource collections hosted by academic institutions where use is already established through OPACs. OCLC's NetFirst, InterCat, and CORC projects, described in Chapter 2, all use LCSH. In some networked resource applications, LCSH application is modified—using only main headings, for example, or main headings and one level of subdivision.

Many Dublin Core projects use LCSH in the subject element, although it may be just one of many possible thesauri. The Australian Government Locator Service (AGLS) *User Manual*, for example, lists LCSH (and four other thesauri) as being in common use across government agencies. The Dublin Core template developed for the Nordic Metadata Project presents LCSH as the default choice for filling in the controlled vocabulary subject element, but the dropdown list of alternatives lists more than 30 other possibilities (see Figure 4.3).

Figure 4.2

Library of Congress Subject Headings

MARC formats—United States—Handbooks, manuals, etc.

Classification—Books—History

Public librarians—Employment—Oklahoma—Bartlesville—
  History—20th century

Academic libraries—Massachusetts—Cambridge—History—
  20th century

Environmental sciences—Vocational guidance

Business enterprises—Communication systems

Medicine, Magic, mystic, and spagiric

Figure 4.3
Controlled Vocabularies in the Nordic Metadata Template

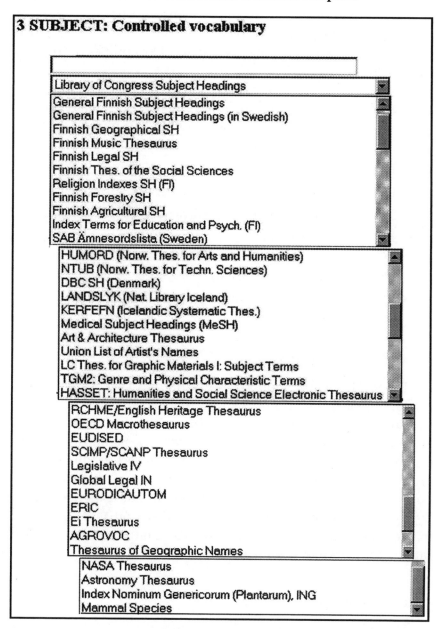

3 SUBJECT: Controlled vocabulary

Library of Congress Subject Headings
General Finnish Subject Headings
General Finnish Subject Headings (in Swedish)
Finnish Geographical SH
Finnish Music Thesaurus
Finnish Legal SH
Finnish Thes. of the Social Sciences
Religion Indexes SH (FI)
Finnish Forestry SH
Finnish Agricultural SH
Index Terms for Education and Psych. (FI)
SAB Ämnesordslista (Sweden)

HUMORD (Norw. Thes. for Arts and Humanities)
NTUB (Norw. Thes. for Techn. Sciences)
DBC SH (Denmark)
LANDSLYK (Nat. Library Iceland)
KERFEFN (Icelandic Systematic Thes.)
Medical Subject Headings (MeSH)
Art & Architecture Thesaurus
Union List of Artist's Names
LC Thes. for Graphic Materials I: Subject Terms
TGM2: Genre and Physical Characteristic Terms
HASSET: Humanities and Social Science Electronic Thesaurus

RCHME/English Heritage Thesaurus
OECD Macrothesaurus
EUDISED
SCIMP/SCANP Thesaurus
Legislative IV
Global Legal IN
EURODICAUTOM
ERIC
Ei Thesaurus
AGROVOC
Thesaurus of Geographic Names

NASA Thesaurus
Astronomy Thesaurus
Index Nominum Genericorum (Plantarum), ING
Mammal Species

INFOMINE

INFOMINE, discussed as an early implementer in Chapter 2, uses LCSH for detailed indexing and also for "meta-subjects"; that is, broad disciplinary headings. Mitchell (1996) outlines the reasons for choosing LCSH:

- A technique was developed for making LCSH indexing efficient and simple (basically cutting and pasting from records in other LCSH-based databases);
- LCSH crosses disciplines;
- LCSH can be both broad and specific;
- The system is familiar to librarians (who provide INFOMINE records);
- LCSH can be supplemented in the future with specialized vocabularies and key words; and
- Records could be compatible with MARC-based systems if this becomes desirable.

Scout Report Signpost

The Scout Report Signpost uses LCSH and LC classification in cataloging electronic resources for a higher education audience. Resources which are fully described (about half of the collection) are assigned from one to five subject headings. Signpost's classification browsing is discussed in Chapter 3. Subject headings can be browsed alphabetically, with links from brief records to full Signpost descriptions (see Figure 4.4). Based on their experience with Signpost, Glassel and Wells (1998) advise that more work is needed in providing suitable LC form subject headings to describe new Internet formats and resources.

eLib Gateways

The subject gateways developed under the U.K. eLib program are singled out here because they use a multiplicity of indexing lan-

Figure 4.4

Subject Headings in Scout Report Signpost

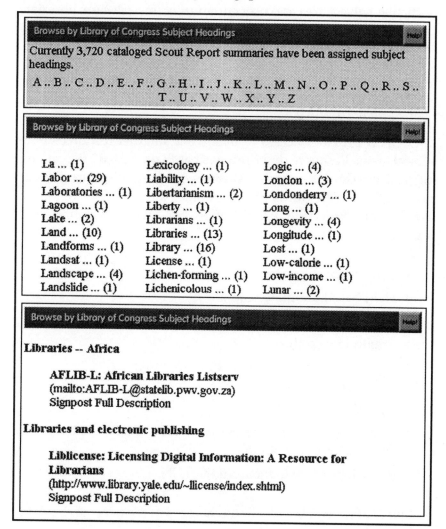

Reprinted with permission.

guages and serve to illustrate a diversity of approaches to controlled vocabulary usage. Most of the gateways use the ROADS software (described in Chapter 3), which provides a framework for the use of classification and controlled vocabulary without stipulating specific schemes, leaving the gateway to determine what is best given the particular subject area and user community. In each case, librarians and technical staff are responsible for selecting, evaluating, and describing the resources which comprise the gateway.

Art, Design, Architecture, & Media Information Gateway (ADAM)

ADAM provides access to over 2,500 Internet resources in its subject areas. Resource description is based on AACR2 for cataloging, and the Getty Research Institute's Art & Architecture Thesaurus (AAT) and Thesaurus of Geographic Names (TGN) for subject indexing and browsing. ADAM offers eight ways of getting to resources:

- Simple search;
- Field-based template search;
- Command search;
- Proximity search;
- Scan by date of addition to the collection;
- Browse by ADAM subject heading (a navigable categorization);
- Browse by ADAM subject heading or AAT term, with time and resource type limits; and
- Browse by place name from the TGN.

A complex faceted classification scheme is at the heart of the AAT, which makes for an interesting approach to browsing. The interface guides the user through AAT facets and arrays, and includes empty nodes—that is, index terms which are part of the full classification, but which have not yet been assigned (see Figure 4.5). *Strategy for*

Figure 4.5

Index Term Navigation in ADAM

Browse by ADAM Subject Heading

Applied Arts
Architecture
Design
Fine Art
General Arts Resources
Media
Museum Studies

Top
  Applied Arts
    Ceramics
    Furniture
    General Applied Arts
    Glass
    Hand Crafts
    Jewellery

Applied Arts
  Ceramics
    Designers and Manufacturers A-Z
    Geographical Area
    History
    Materials
    Organisations
    Resource Type
    Techniques
    Theory and Criticism

1.   **Clayzee: Worldwide Ceramics and Pottery Directory**

Historical Period:

| Any | ▼ |

Resource Type:

| Any | ▼ |

Art & Architecture Thesaurus

Top
  Built Complexes and Districts
    complexes
    districts

ADAM Subject Headings	Art & Architecture Thesaurus
Applied Arts	Associated Concepts
Architecture	Attributes and Properties
Design	Built Complexes and
Fine Art	Districts
General Arts	Color
Resources	Components

Reprinted with permission.

the Use of Vocabulary in the ADAM Database (1996) reveals some of the decision making in choosing the AAT and choosing against Dewey, and considers the problems of making a classification scheme into a textual category listing.

Organizing Medical Networked Information (OMNI)

OMNI, hosted at the University of Nottingham, covers medicine, biomedicine, health services, and related topics. By the end of 1999, the OMNI gateway included close to 4,500 descriptive records. Searchable fields include titles, descriptions, and keywords chosen from the U.S. National Library of Medicine (NLM) medical subject headings list (MeSH). In addition to direct search, users can browse through resources using an alphabetical or notational list of sections from the NLM classification scheme (OMNI's use of classification is described in Chapter 3) and can also browse the MeSH thesaurus. Thesaurus browse leads to a display which shows the subject heading, related terms (derived from NLM's Unified Medical Language System metathesaurus), and resources indexed by the specific heading (see Figure 4.6).

Social Science Information Gateway (SOSIG)

SOSIG is hosted at the University of Bristol, and focuses on social science education and research. SOSIG uses the Humanities and Social Science Electronic Thesaurus (HASSET), developed at the University of Essex, for subject indexing. Of particular interest here, the thesaurus-browsing capability shows broader, narrower, and related terms for adding to a search or for further thesaurus navigation (see Figure 4.7).

California Environmental Resources Evaluation System (CERES)

CERES, developed by the California Resources Agency, brings together California-related electronic environmental information from a variety of public, educational, and private sources. CERES

Figure 4.6

Thesaurus Browse in OMNI

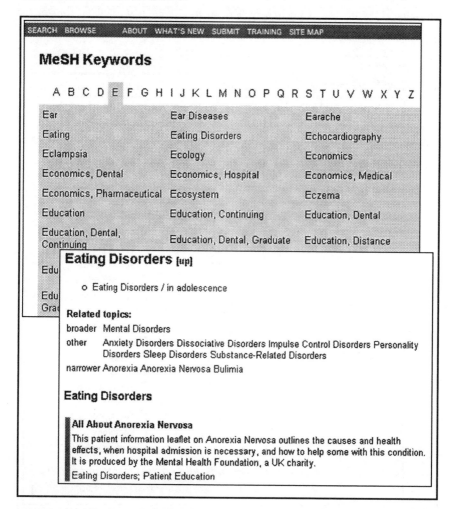

Reprinted with permission.

Figure 4.7

The HASSETT Thesaurus in SOSIG

Use the HASSET Thesaurus to provide alternative terms that will generate hits within the SOSIG Internet Catalogue.

social welfare   Look Up Thesaurus

Help on the HASSET Thesaurus

To search the SOSIG Catalogue for one or more terms, check the terms required and click on the Search SOSIG Catalogue button below.
To explore the Thesaurus further, select a hyperlinked term.

Current term:

☐ **social welfare**

Broader terms:	Narrower terms:	Related terms:
none	☐ educational welfare	☐ social action
	☐ social services	☐ social justice
	☐ social work	☐ social needs
		☐ social problems
		☐ social responsibility
		☐ social welfare administration
		☐ social welfare finance
		☐ social welfare organizations
		☐ social welfare philosophy
		☐ social workers
		☐ sociology
		☐ welfare policy

Include all narrower terms in search ☐

Search SOSIG Catalogue

Reprinted with permission.

has developed metadata catalogs and standards, and encourages collaboration by sharing tools to support resource contribution. The CERES Catalog DTD is based on the Federal Geographic Data Committee's (FGDC) Content Standards for Digital Geospatial Metadata (CSDGM) and, to some degree, the National Biological Survey's (NBS) Draft Content Standard for Non-Geospatial Metadata. CERES information access includes information sorted by organization, geographic area (with a map interface), theme, and data type. The last two go to a thesaurus browser at the head of a list of keywords. Choosing a keyword from the list or entering a direct search opens up options in the thesaurus browser to find similar words and to show a hierarchy surrounding the keyword (see Figure 4.8).

CONCERNS ABOUT CONTROLLED VOCABULARIES

A wealth of experience in working with LCSH-based catalogs, and a large body of research into how users interact with alphabetical subject access systems in OPACs and other settings, has implications for networked resource collections which are modeled on the same tools and systems. In her most recent research, Drabenstott, who has published an influential body of work on subject access and online catalogs, reports on a large-scale examination of whether and how users understand subject headings—the overall finding indicated that in many cases they do not (Drabenstott, Simcox, & Fenton, 1999). In an introduction to a collection of research articles on OPACs, Beaulieu and Borgman (1996) point out that "research continues to show that these systems are ineffective and hard to use" (p. 491).

Roe (1999) summarizes research findings on subject access problems in OPACs and general Web searching:

- "No items retrieved";
- "Too many items retrieved";
- "Only unrelated items retrieved";
- "Retrieval of some, but not all or the best sources"; and

Figure 4.8

CERES Thesaurus Browser

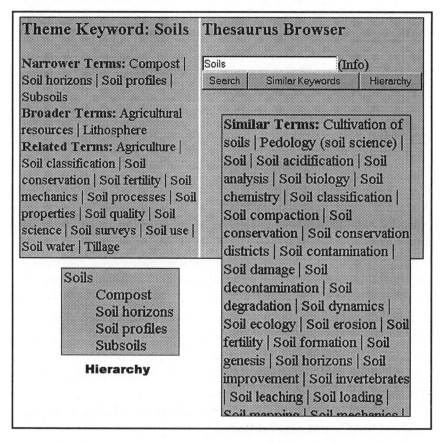

- "As the user switches from database to database or Website to Website the vocabulary used to express their search becomes more varied and the "Tower of Babel" effect takes over." (p. 71)

She goes on to characterize some of the recommended solutions to these problems, including linking statistically derived indexing to controlled vocabularies, providing the user with more access to underlying control structures, and developing mechanisms for cross-vocabulary switching or mapping.

Bates (1998) identifies some of the fundamental problems in subject access. Some of these are related to human factors and the disjunction between indexers and users. An indexer has a document in hand and expertise in using what may be a complex indexing language. Users have vaguely stated information needs, no idea as to whether one or more pertinent documents exist, and little or no awareness or understanding of the indexing language. This is especially a problem in the online world, where information seeking is protracted and iterative, and requirements change during the process as a consequence of seeing intermediate search results. Koll's (1998) "haystack" slide (see Figure 4.9), characterizing the kinds of questions users take to search engines, highlights the problem. Bates also points out that human expression is richly varied, and no matter how rich an entry vocabulary, it is extremely difficult to predict the terms with which a user will characterize a topic of interest. This again makes the case for more attention to the concept of the searching thesaurus.

The reasons for failure in subject searching are not completely understood, and a variety of solutions have been proposed—some suggest changes in the structure and application of indexing languages, others look to changes in the interface. What is important is that designers of subject access systems need to understand the limitations, stay abreast of current research which may suggest means for improvement, and be open to experimentation with new methods and technologies.

The interest in the application of controlled vocabularies has certainly not diminished with the advent of networked resource

Figure 4.9

Finding a Needle in a Haystack

A *known* needle in a *known* haystack

A *known* needle in a *unknown* haystack

An *unknown* needle in an *unknown* haystack

Any needle in a haystack

The *sharpest* needle in a haystack

Most of the *sharpest* needles in a haystack

All the needles in a haystack

Affirmation of *no needles* in the haystack

Things *like* needles in any haystack

Let me know *whenever* a new needle shows up

Where are the *haystacks?*

Needles, haystacks—*whatever*

Source: Adapted from Koll (1998). Reprinted with permission of Matthew Koll.

databases. Metadata developments such as the Dublin Core, XML, and the RDF, described in Chapter 2, support indexing language applications. A Z39.50 profile for thesaurus navigation has been proposed (M. Taylor, 1999). Topics proposed for a 1999 meeting of the Networked Knowledge Organization Systems (NKOS) group included RDF and NKOS, distributed thesaurus standards, thesaurus linkages, and use scenarios (Hill, 1999), and the group is collectively working on metadata for knowledge organizing system (KOS) registries.

General resource discovery through search engines leaves much to be desired, and while subject gateways are successful, they represent only a small proportion of the Internet. Koch and Vizine-Goetz's (1999) observation that "services of each type recognize the benefits of their counterparts and are increasingly adopting each other's features" bodes well for the future of structured subject access, although the tools and applications may undergo some profound reshaping.

REFERENCES

Aitchison, Jean, Gilchrist, Alan, & Bawden, David. (1997). *Thesaurus construction and use: A practical manual* (3rd ed.). London: Aslib.

Anderson, James D. (1997). *Guidelines for indexing and related information retrieval devices* (NISO Technical Report 2; NISO TR02-1977). Bethesda, MD: NISO Press.

Anderson, James D., & Rowley, Frederick A. (1992). Building end-user thesauri from full-text. *Advances in Classification Research, 2*, 1–13.

Austin, Derek. (1974). The development of PRECIS: A theoretical and technical history. *Journal of Documentation, 30*, 47–102.

Bates, Marcia J. (1989). Rethinking subject cataloging in the online environment. *Library Resources & Technical Services, 33*, 400–412.

Bates, Marcia J. (1998). Indexing and access for digital libraries and the Internet: Human, database, and domain factors. *Journal of the American Society for Information Science, 49*, 1185–1205.

Beaulieu, Micheline, & Borgman, Christine L. (1996). A new era for OPAC research: Introduction to special issue on current research in online public access systems. *Journal of the American Society for Information Science, 47*, 491–492.

Chan, Lois Mai. (1990). *Library of Congress subject headings: Principles of structure and policies for application.* Washington, DC: Library of Congress, Cataloging Distribution Service.

Chan, Lois Mai. (1994). *Cataloguing and classification: An introduction* (2nd ed.). New York: McGraw-Hill.

Chan, Lois Mai. (1995). *Library of Congress subject headings: Principles and application* (3rd ed.). Englewood, CO: Libraries Unlimited.

Chan, Lois Mai, Richmond, Phyllis A., & Svenonius, Elaine. (1985). *Theory of subject analysis: A sourcebook.* Englewood, CO: Libraries Unlimited.

Coates, Eric James. (1960). *Subject catalogues: Headings and structure.* London: Library Association.

Cochrane, Pauline A. (1992). Indexing and searching thesauri: The Janus or Proteus of information retrieval. In N.J. Williamson & H. Hudon (Eds.), *Classification research for knowledge representation and organization: Proceedings of the 5th International Study Conference on Classification Research, Toronto, Canada, 24–28 June, 1991* (pp. 161–177). Amsterdam, Netherlands: Elsevier.

Cutter, Charles Ammi. (1904). *Rules for a dictionary catalog* (4th ed.). Washington, DC: U.S. GPO.

Drabenstott, Karen M., Simcox, Schelle, & Fenton, Eileen G. (1999). End-user understanding of subject headings in library catalogs. *Library Resources & Technical Services, 43,* 140–160.

Foskett, Anthony Charles. (1996). *The subject approach to information* (5th ed.). London: Library Association.

Glassel, Aimee, & Wells, Amy Tracy. (1998). Scout Report Signpost: Design and development for access to cataloged Internet resources. *Journal of Internet Cataloging, 1*(3), 15–45.

Hill, Linda L. (1999, February 16). Proposal for ACM DL'99 workshop. In *NKOS listserv archive.* Retrieved January 4, 2000 from the World Wide Web: http://orc.dev.oclc.org:5103/nkos/msg00050.html.

International Organization for Standardization. (1986). *Documentation: Guidelines for the establishment and development of monolingual thesauri* (ISO 2788:1986 (E)). Geneva, Switzerland: International Organization for Standardization.

International Organization for Standardization. (1996). *Information and documentation: Guidelines for the content, organization and presentation of indexes* (ISO 999:1996). Geneva, Switzerland: International Organization for Standardization.

Koch, Traugott, & Vizine-Goetz, Diane. (1999, June 16). *Automatic classification and content navigation support for Web services: DESIRE II cooperates with OCLC*. Retrieved January 4, 2000 from the World Wide Web: http://www.oclc.org/oclc/research/publications/review98/koch_vizine-goetz/automatic.htm.

Koll, Matt. (1998). History and state-of-the-art of the statistical approach search engines. Paper presented at *Search engines and beyond: A landmark conference*. Retrieved January 3, 2000 from the World Wide Web: http://www.infonortics.com/searchengines/boston1998/koll/sld010.htm.

Lancaster, F.W. (1972). *Vocabulary control for information retrieval*. Washington, DC: Information Resources Press.

Lancaster, F.W. (1986). *Vocabulary control for information retrieval* (2nd ed.). Washington, DC: Information Resources Press.

Lancaster, F.W. (1998). *Indexing and abstracting in theory and practice* (2nd ed.). Champaign: University of Illinois, Graduate School of Library & Information Science.

Library of Congress, Cataloging Policy and Support Office. (1996). *Subject cataloging manual: Subject headings*. Washington, DC: Library of Congress, Cataloging Distribution Service.

Metcalfe, John Wallace. (1957). *Information indexing and subject cataloging: Alphabetical, classified, coordinate, mechanical*. New York: Scarecrow Press.

Mitchell, Steve. (1996, April 29). *Library of Congress subject headings as subject terminology in a virtual library: The INFOMINE example*. Retrieved December 29, 1999 from the World Wide Web: http://infomine.ucr.edu/pubs/postlcsh.html.

National Information Standards Organization. (1994). *Guidelines for the construction, format, and management of monolingual thesauri* (ANSI/NISO Z39.19-1993). Bethesda, MD: NISO Press.

Ranganathan, Shiyali Ramamrita. (1967). *Prolegomena to library classification* (3rd ed.). New York: Asia Publishing House.

Roe, Sandy. (1999). Online subject access. *Journal of Internet Cataloging, 2*(1), 69–78.

Rowley, Jennifer. (1994). The controlled versus natural indexing languages debate revisited: A perspective on information retrieval practice and research. *Journal of Information Science, 20*, 108–119.

Schatz, Bruce R., Johnson, Eric H., & Cochrane, Pauline A. (1996). Interactive term suggestion for users of digital libraries: Using subject the-

sauri and co-occurrence lists for information retrieval. In E.A. Fox
& G. Marchionini (Eds.), *Proceedings of the 1st ACM International
Conference on Digital Libraries* (pp. 126–133). New York: Association
for Computing Machinery.

Soergel, Dagobert. (1974). *Indexing languages and thesauri: Construction and
maintenance.* Los Angeles: Melville.

Soergel, Dagobert. (1994). Indexing and retrieval performance: The logical
evidence. *Journal of the American Society for Information Science, 45,*
589–599.

Stevens, Mary Elizabeth, Giuliano, Vincent E., & Heilprin, Laurence B. (Eds.).
(1965). *Statistical association methods for mechanized documentation:
Symposium proceedings.* Washington, DC: U.S. GPO.

Strategy for the use of vocabulary in the ADAM database. (1996). Retrieved
December 30, 1999 from the World Wide Web: http://adam.ac.uk/
adam/public/SF1f9605.rtf.

Taylor, Arlene G. (1999). *The organization of information.* Englewood, CO:
Libraries Unlimited.

Taylor, Arlene G. (2000). *Introduction to cataloging and classification* (9th ed.).
Englewood, CO: Libraries Unlimited.

Taylor, Mike. (1999, February 28). *Zthes: A Z39.50 profile for thesaurus navigation.* Retrieved January 4, 2000 from the World Wide Web:
http://lcweb.loc.gov/z3950/agency/profiles/zthes-02.html.

WEB PAGE

Vocabulary control et al. http://www.simmons.edu/~schwartz/myalpha.
html.

5

Search Engines

The term "search engine," as used by the average visitor to the World Wide Web, encompasses a wide variety of services which provide access to Internet resources. In the field of information retrieval research, a distinction is made between the interface and the engine—the former is the means by which the user interacts with the latter. Not so to Jane or John Q. Surfer, to whom the concept of search engine includes the interface, the retrieval and presentation mechanism, and the database. In common with library catalogs, users of Internet search engines are concerned with results, rarely understand or even consider the mechanisms, and even more rarely make full use of the capabilities provided by sophisticated search tools. Pollock and Hockley's (1997) study of search engine use by Internet-naïve adults (whether computer-literate or otherwise) certainly backs this up. Those subjects misunderstood what the Internet is, what types of resources it contains, why searches might require several iterations, and what types of keywords might be fruitful, and even lacked sufficient basic knowledge to be able to recognize "answers."

Unlike library catalogs, most publicly available search services on the Web (apart from those provided in digital library environments) are funded by advertising dollars, and the effort to draw customers (i.e., searchers) to a particular "portal" tends to emphasize packaging over product (Berst, 1998). It appears to be the case that most people find one or two search engines which they like, often for reasons to do with ease of use or speed of response, and that they become loyal customers (see, for instance, the survey by Stobart & Kerridge, 1996). To promote that brand loyalty, search engine providers pay inordinately large fees to be the service which is linked to a browser button labeled "search" (Andrews, 1998). In fact, some engines even pay for use. It also seems that most casual users use one or two words to drive a search (McLaughlin, 1999). Despite this, many search services now provide an array of search tools approaching those available in the realm of commercial online searching (except for the enhancements provided by indexing languages and authority control).

BACKGROUND

The Internet became widely available to the scholarly (and eventually business and consumer) community as a research and communication tool toward the end of the 1980s. The discovery process for access to the resources provided under each newly available function (beginning with telnet, and FTP, and moving through listservs, news groups, Gopher, WAIS and the Web) frequently began with word of mouth or, more commonly, word of e-mail—colleague telling colleague about some new file or site. Printed directories of electronic discussion groups, e-journals, telnet-accessible services, and so on were published, but print publishing has never been a particularly appropriate method for keeping up to date with Internet resources.

Fortunately, each function was also followed quite quickly by the deployment of one or more electronic discovery devices. Files available via anonymous FTP could be found using archie. Listserv archives could be searched via commands sent to the server. Online directories such as HYTELNET and LIBS pointed to libraries and other collections that could be reached with telnet. Widespread adoption of Gopher in the early 1990s was attended by the development of veronica, and then jughead, both of which provided keyword search through the text of Gopher menu lines and could be used within the confines of one site or on information gathered from all of Gopher space. WAIS was somewhat different. Developed by Brewster Kahle, then at Thinking Machines, Inc., WAIS drew from work on two fronts: 30 years of research in the information science community on using statistical characteristics of text for retrieval, and more recent developments in the library community on the Z39.50 protocol for interoperability between multitype automated library catalogs. Public WAIS sites presented directories of collections available for search, and search through specified collections resulted in a list of files ranked primarily on the basis of search term occurrence.

The year 1991 saw the first general release of WWW line-mode browsers at CERN (the European Lab for Particle Physics). Windows and Macintosh graphical browsers arrived in 1993, and the subsequent rapid growth of the World Wide Web is well documented (Calliau, 1995; Gray, 1998; Zakon, 1998). There is little agreement as to the actual number of Web resources available on servers around the world, but the word "overwhelming" is usually considered apt. In the early days, when servers were few and knowledge of markup rare, resource discovery started at the CERN Web site, which included an alphabetized subject listing of links to pages forming the World Wide Web Virtual Library (the opening CERN page as it appeared on November 3, 1992, has been archived at http://www.w3.org/History/19921103-hypertext/hypertext/WWW/TheProject.html).

In 1994, as the number of Web resources increased, the services that we now know as search engines began to appear. Most seem to have started as research (or recreation) projects undertaken by graduate students, faculty, systems staff, and other "Web-heads." Some projects fell by the wayside as the task began to exceed the capacity of limited human and technical resources; most of those that survived were either acquired by corporations, financed by advertising and capital investment, or funded by research initiatives. By 1996, search engines began to be featured in trade journals, and then in business and daily newspapers, and magazines such as *Scientific*

American (Lynch, 1997) and *Science* (Lawrence & Giles, 1998), and in news clips and commercials on network television. Differentiated search products proliferated—search engine directories, meta-engines, subject-specific services, personal desktop search agents, and "push" (automated current awareness) services. Like the Web, the world of search services is now complex, rich, volatile, and frequently frustrating.

SEARCH ENGINES TODAY

Types of Search Services

There are two basic search engine types: classified lists, of which Yahoo is the best-known example, and query-based engines, which are far more common (e.g., AltaVista, Excite, and Infoseek). Both maintain databases containing representations of Web pages (and sometimes other resources) in some form. Classified lists present arrays of resource links in systematically arranged categories, often quite complex hierarchies. Query-based engines run search algorithms based on user-input text expressions. Classified lists usually allow query-based search of category labels and resource titles, and query-based services often provide browseable categories as well, but it is generally obvious that a search engine is primarily of one kind or the other.

Web users and researchers (especially librarians and other information professionals) being who they are, it is not surprising that aids have been developed to cope with the proliferation of general search services and the availability of numerous specialized services. These aids include directories and meta-engines. Directories, such as Search Engine Guide (see Figure 5.1), are lists of search engines, usually organized into useful categories (e.g., searching for people or companies). Some directories simply provide links, many provide input boxes so that queries can be sent directly to selected engines, and some provide detailed annotations about scope and search features.

A meta-engine sends a query to more than one search engine (as many as 20 or 30), sometimes of the user's choosing. Results may be

Figure 5.1

Search Engine Guide

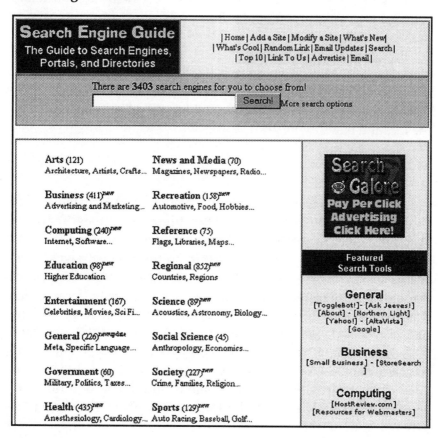

Reprinted with permission.

merged, with duplicates removed (e.g., MetaCrawler, the first meta-engine, shown in Figure 5.2), or may be presented as separate lists from each engine (All4One, for example, displays results from each engine in a separate frame, seen in Figure 5.3). While most meta-engines are sites on the Web, personal search agents such as Intelliseek's BullsEye and GO.com's Express Search are desktop examples. Newer tools like Flyswat, Kenjin, and WebCheck search networked content (on the Web or in locally held or proprietary sources) for material related to user-selected text from almost any desktop application.

Browsers have entered the search service foray as well. Both Netscape and Microsoft Internet Explorer offer "what's related" searches, using Alexa-based software to suggest sites related to the current one, and both provide searching directly from input into the location bar.

Search Service Content

It is usually possible to submit a Web page to a search service for inclusion in the indexed database of representations. There are Web sites which facilitate this process, and most search services provide a "submit your URL" procedure on their home pages. Most search services also acquire database information from Web pages through the use of agents, or robots, which retrieve URLs and then representation data from the 'Net, following link paths and seeking new or changed resources. For example, AltaVista's Web spider collects data on many millions of Web pages daily. The frequency with which a database is refreshed with new or changed information varies—the Search Engine Watch site includes a section (for subscribers only) which charts the frequency with which search engines drop in on sites.

Agents trawling the Web automatically on behalf of search services can learn to re-examine frequently sites which change a great deal or to which many other pages link. Alternatively, they may emphasize resources which are "isolated," that is, not referenced by many other pages. When retrieving one URL among a complex collection of inter- and intralinked pages, an agent can mark the site

Figure 5.2

MetaCrawler

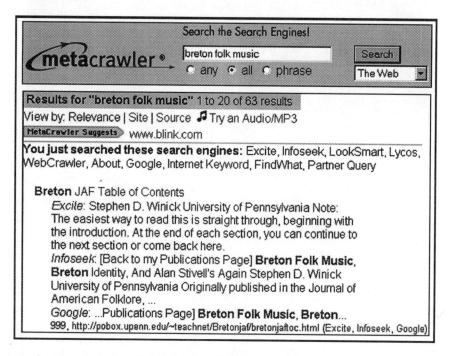

Figure 5.3

All4One

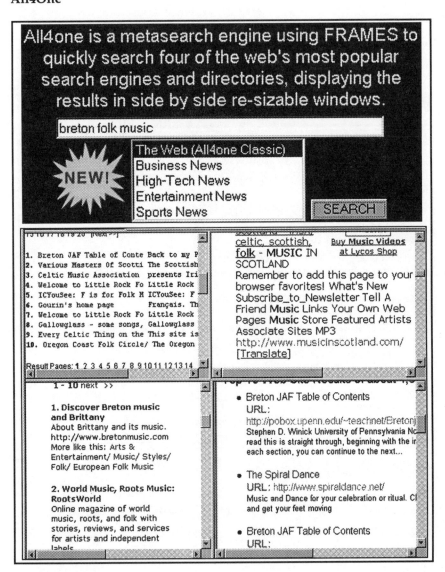

Reprinted with permission.

for re-examination, to acquire at a later point information about all or a sampling of the remaining pages. Robot strategies for following complex interdocument links are generally based on the assumption that Web sites are arranged hierarchically or at least logically (e.g., shorter path names should reflect superordinate pages), an assumption which can lead to failure to collect key materials (Smith, Moxley, & Maze, 1997). Also, use of frames, imagemaps, programming through CGI or Java, XML, and so on can impede the progress of some agents in the "trawling" process. Lawrence and Giles (1998) estimated that even the largest of search engines covers only a fraction of the Web. Kochtanek et al. (1998) studied five search engines for their indexing of a multipage test site. They found differences with respect to when and how frequently the site was visited, which pages were examined, and whether and how terms were extracted for representations.

Classified list services review submitted or harvested information for inclusion. Subject-specialized search services or "vortals" (vertical market portals) such as LawCrawler also engage in an intellectual selection process to maintain content quality, and use tailored agents to limit discovery to appropriate resources. Some general-content query services reduce the size of the haystack by establishing subset databases of selected and reviewed resources or most popular ones. Some provide proprietary, and perhaps fee-based, information sources. In addition to indexing HTML pages, many query-based services include Usenet news (a limited timespan) and Gopher menus, and some harvest and index a wider variety of formats, such as ASCII, SGML, Virtual Reality Modelling Language (VRML), and Portable Document File (PDF).

The roster of indexed elements in the representation varies from service to service. Some services index every word on a page (in some cases including the URL), ALT text in the HTML image tag, and comment text. Positional and markup tag information may be stored with indexed text to improve retrieval and ranking effectiveness. Others index only frequently occurring words, or only words occurring within certain markup tags, or only the first so many words or lines of HTML files. Stopwords may or be not be applied, either in retrieval or in ranking, and if applied may include content-bearing words of very high frequency, such as "web," "internet," "html," and so on (Feldman, 1998). Representations might (rarely) be enhanced by the intellectual addition of keywords, category terms, or (even more rarely) reviews and summaries, all of which may contribute to retrieval but have a negative effect on timeliness in that they require human intervention.

Search Features

The opening screen of a typical query-based search engine presents an input box (which has been shrinking in size as advertising and "try this first" sections increase) and possibly a choice as to how the query terms are to be processed (e.g., "any/all/this exact phrase"). The implicit Boolean operator between query terms may be assumed to be an OR or an AND, depending on the search engine, and several search engines will try to extract query phrases for searching. Defaults with respect to automatic stemming, case sensitivity, matching to irregular plurals or alternate forms (e.g., "jail" and "gaol"), fields being searched, stopwords, and so on are rarely obvious, even to searchers who might want to know. Many search engines provide a full array of sophisticated search commands, but the casual user is usually protected from these by their being in a help file or only accessible under the guise of "power" or "advanced" search. Figure 5.4 shows the simple and advanced search screens in FAST.

Common advanced capabilities (although one suspects that they are rarely used) include:

- Boolean search (in some cases with nested parentheses);
- Specification of terms which must or must not be present;
- Truncation (terminal and internal) or, conversely, inhibition of automatic stemming;
- Exact phrase match;
- Proximity searching (which can be as sophisticated as that found in commercial online searching);

Figure 5.4

Simple and Advanced Search in FAST

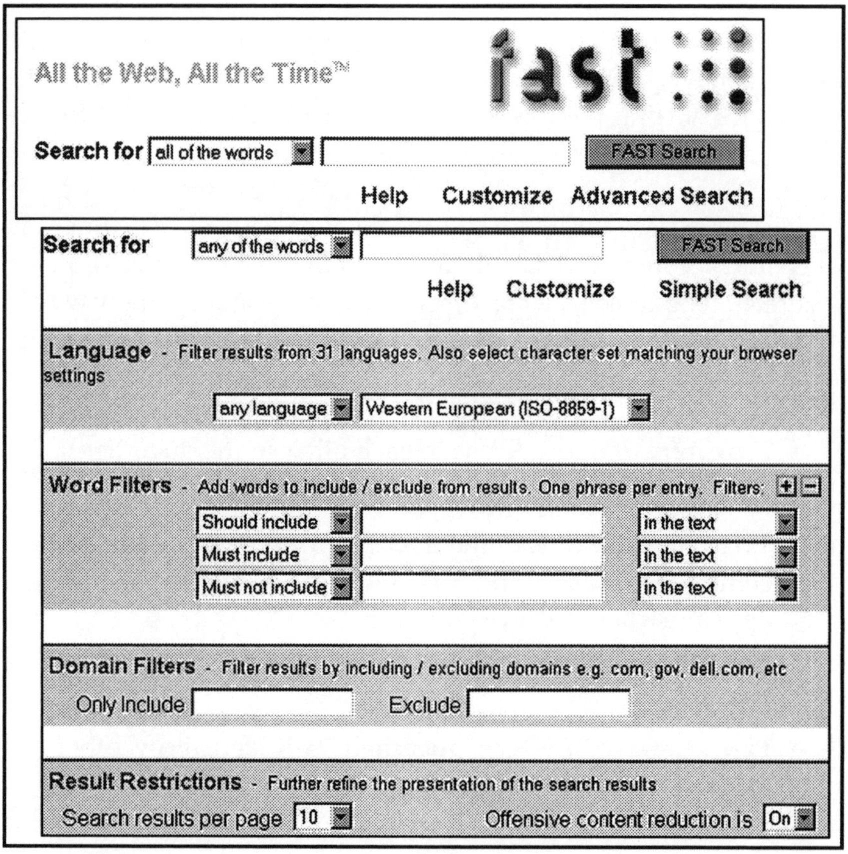

Reprinted with permission.

- Fielded search (e.g., based on markup tags identifying title text, meta text, heading text, link, etc.);
- Specification as to case sensitivity; and
- Restriction by date, domain, language, or file type (based on file name extension).

Search Results

Although experience with search engines sometimes makes this hard to believe, search results are usually ranked by relevance, with options for sorting the top of the list instead by site (useful for reducing duplication) or (rarely) by date. Being proprietary, the means by which ranking is accomplished are seldom described in any great detail. At the very least, query term frequency in the document is taken into account, and calculations may involve normalization for document length (i.e., the fact that a document contains many words is taken into account in consideration of the frequency of occurrence of a single word). Additional possible parameters include:

- Proximity of query terms to each other in the document;
- Frequency of query term across the database;
- Term location in the document (with higher weight assigned to <TITLE> and <META> text or to terms which appear earlier in the document);
- Term location in the query (earlier terms being more important);
- Frequency with which document is linked to by other documents in the database;
- Popularity of document with previous searchers looking for similar information; and
- Whether or not the document forms part of the "reviewed" content provided by the search service.

Word spamming (embedding repeated terms in <META> tags or elsewhere for purposes of promoting high rank) is penalized by several search engines. Some engines allow the user to participate in ranking decisions by, for instance, specifying the strength of match, the number of terms to be matched, and so on. Unfortunately, many search services have removed these options, probably owing to lack of use by most searchers.

Most search engines present results 10 or so at a time, in a default format showing title and some text, and accompanied by a cheery message along the lines of "1–10 of 69010." Both the number of hits per page and the format display can usually be changed. Format displays can include any of the following:

- Title;
- Relevance score (expressed in a variety of scales);
- Summary (summaries may be prepared abstracts, outlines created by extracting text in headings tags, most frequent words, the first so many words, or some automatically constructed representation);
- File size in bytes;
- File date;
- Date of entry into the database;
- URL;
- Language;
- Category label (if the search service includes a classified array); and
- Search terms present in the resource.

Additional elements may be included with results displays. Many services provide a relevance feedback option, using high-frequency terms from the identified relevant document to restate the query, and quite a few engines group pages from the same site. For example, the last line of GO.com's Infoseek results includes "find similar pages," "more results [from this site]," and even "translate this page."

All of these devices are intended to help searchers make sense of results, but still the product of a query in current search engine circumstances is often poorly ordered and bewildering. Realizing this, most search services and many searchers (especially information specialists) have put together collections of "search tips." These are distilled in the appendix to this chapter.

STUDYING SEARCH ENGINES

The body of work on Web search engines is already quite extensive. Print and electronic trade literature (and Web resources) in the information and financial industries feature product announcements and discussions of the business aspects of managing and financing search services. Search engine guides, feature tables, and practical tips are published in professional journals or mounted on the Web by libraries, search service companies, and individuals with an interest in searching. Journals and conference proceedings in computer science, engineering, library and information science, and related fields carry performance comparisons and research reports on new work in networked information retrieval. Sullivan's Search Engine Watch site holds a wealth of original content as well as collections of links to print and electronic sources on Web search services. *Online* columnist Greg Notess' Search Engine Showdown is somewhat similar, but slanted to the information professional. Textbooks have made an appearance, beginning with Maze, Moxley, and Smith's (1997) fine explanation of the technology behind search engines, with details on how to get the most out of the best known, and followed by a number of texts on searching generally (e.g., Ackermann & Hartman, 1999; Bradley, 1999; Gould, 1998; Hock, 1999) or in specific subject areas (e.g., Bates, 1999; Paul & Williams, 1999).

Performance Evaluation

Search service comparisons abound, and most consist principally of feature charts. These are useful in themselves, but date very quickly and do not say much about retrieval performance. Information industry Web sites and trade publications publish some performance ratings, although in most cases the methods of assessment and evaluation are either unspecified or unsystematic. ZDNet held several "search engine showdowns" (Lake, 1997) and publishes regular surveys and ratings (see, for example, Lidsky & Sirapyan, 1999)— the showdown testers are business people who use the Internet, and the queries show some complexity, but this is not "research" such as one might find in the information retrieval literature. CNET, *Internet World*, *PC Magazine*, and similar agencies regularly carry lab tests, ratings, and feature charts (Haskin, 1997; Home on the Web, 1998; Keizer, 1998).

Search engine comparisons by and for information professionals display more depth. Courtois, Baer, and Stark (1995) assessed seven services based on "known-URL" searches. Feldman (1997) tested precision in seven search engines using real user queries for information about companies, products, medical data, foreign information, technical reports, and current events. Text and links in the first 10 retrieved items were examined for relevance. Peterson (1997) compared eight search engines for the results of two queries repeated in three time periods. Kimmel (1996) performed simple searches in nine engines, mostly to examine coverage and compare features. Westera (1997) used queries of different types (single keyword, plural keyword, phrase, Boolean, and proper name) and replicated her tests six months apart in time. In one of the best examples of this type of comparison, Zorn, Emanoil, Marshall, and Panek (1996) used three complex Boolean searches across four search engines to illustrate a comparison of advanced features, indexing depth, and quality of help. While the low number of queries and other design factors preclude any valid statistical analysis, the in-depth discussion of search results is illuminating.

Chu and Rosenthal (1996) evaluated AltaVista, Lycos, and Excite using 10 queries derived from reference questions and using available command features for each engine. Relevance judgments for the first 10 results from each engine formed the basis for precision calculations. In the context of developing a meta-engine, Gauch and Wang (1996) calculated a "confidence factor" for six search engines based on 25 queries, taking into account not only precision in the first 10 results but also ranking accuracy. Schlichting and Nilsen's (1996) work evaluated AltaVista, Excite, Infoseek, and Lycos based on searches using from four to six keywords gathered from topics submitted by academic faculty. The first 10 results across search engines were merged and scored by subjects using a seven-point scale for useful items (this is one of the few studies to use user rather than researcher relevance assessments). Search engine ratings incorporated not only relevant and non-relevant retrieved, but also relevant and non-relevant missed.

Ding and Marchionini (1996) compared Infoseek, Lycos, and Open Text for precision, duplication, link validation, and degree of overlap. Five complex queries were run against each engine, and relevance judgments were made for the first 20 results, using a six-point scale. The study by Tomaiuolo and Packer (1996) is notable for its sheer scale—high-precision searches for 200 topics gathered from a reference desk in an undergraduate setting and searched on AltaVista, Infoseek, Lycos, Magellan, and Point. Precision was calculated for the first 10, and the researchers rather than users assessed relevance. Rather than looking solely at retrieval, Xie, Wang, and Goh (1998) used the SERVQUAL framework to identify and measure a broader set of dimensions of quality (from the user point of view) for six popular search engines.

Leighton and Srivastava (1999) express a concern for the presence of bias and lack of statistical validity in most search engine performance evaluation, and attempt to overcome these shortcomings in their study of AltaVista, Excite, HotBot, Infoseek, and Lycos. Fifteen queries, most of which were actual reference desk questions, were input (in most cases) as unstructured text. Each query was run against all engines on the same day, and the first 20 results were merged and "blinded" (i.e., search engine identification was removed). Active links in the results were scored for relevance on a four-point scale. Results are presented with detailed explanations, and the analysis examines the effects of collapsing the relevance scale, weighting for item position in the list, adjusting for when results were fewer than 20, and penalizing for duplicates. To simulate a typical test collection, Clarke and Willett (1997) pooled top-10 relevant search results from three search engines and then searched for the presence of each relevant item (whether or not in the top 10) in all three. This was done for 30 queries, and the results were analyzed for precision, recall, and coverage (the proportion of relevant pages indexed by an engine).

The performance evaluation literature is growing, although reviews of the evaluation literature by Dong and Su (1997) and Su (1997) note the absence of a systematic approach, point out the lack of consistency between researchers in choosing what to measure and how to measure it, and lament the absence of the end user from most such studies. Investigations are largely concerned with precision, since true recall is somewhat difficult in a Web environment. For that matter true precision is elusive as well, given search results on the order of several thousand ranked items. Most studies take a practical "first-10" or "first-20" approach, assessing relevance only for the top of the ranked list, and in most cases researchers rather than users make relevance judgments. Even so, there is something to be said for attempting more than a comparison of features and a personal interpretation of effectiveness based on a small sample.

The purpose of almost all evaluation literature is to determine the best engine. The outcomes usually indicate that differences in performance among the best two or three are not large and that different engines serve different search purposes. In any event, search engines introduce new features so frequently that many observations are almost obsolete by the time they are published. In their excellent summary of search service comparisons and evaluations, Barry and Richardson (1996) tabulate extracts from conclusions drawn in 11 different studies—the general gist is that no one service is "best," and that serious searchers should routinely use more than one. Five years later this still holds true.

User Studies

Studies of user behavior in Web searching began to emerge in the late 1990s. Pollock and Hockley's (1997) study, discussed above, was actually conducted in 1995, and one expects that users might be more Web-savvy by the end of the decade. Su, Chen, and Dong (1998) examined searching by 11 users using four search engines and analyzed relevance, efficiency, utility (related to system features and the value of search results), user satisfaction, and connectivity (link validity). Wang et al. (1998) looked at searching by 24 graduate students to assess general search success and the impact of knowledge and experience, cognitive style, and affective state (stress and anxiety). In a research project exploring affective and cognitive functions, Nahl (1998) used ethnographic techniques to analyze self-reports written by undergraduate novice searchers. Spink, Bateman, and Jansen (1998, 1999) analyzed responses to an interactive survey by 316 Excite users over five days. In addition to general demographic data, they asked about search topics, search terms (an average of 3.34 per user), use of system features such as Boolean operators (use was low), pattern of use of Excite, and results of previous searching activities. Their findings have been supplemented by analysis of over 50,000 queries created by more than 18,000 Excite users (Jansen, Spink, & Saracevic, 2000). Vaughan (1999) studied the factors which influence information professionals' choice of Internet search tools and found that the primary concern was to retrieve the greatest number of useful results, even though that might mean sifting through volumes of irrelevant material.

TRENDS

Even several years later, one has to agree with Berghel that "search engines as they now exist represent a primitive, first cut at efficient information access on the Internet" (1997, p. 20). Berghel goes on to say that the fault lies not so much with search engines, but with the characteristics of the resources which they attempt to index, which he describes as "more wheat than chaff" (p. 21). He is not the first to suggest that exploring alternative methods for networked information discovery may be more fruitful than refining search engines. Berghel's alternatives include information agents, information customization, information providers whose "brands" are associated with value-added resource description and access, and push services. Larsen (1997) agrees that there is only so much to be accomplished by tweaking search engines, which after all evolved from a world where documents are generally homogeneous and well structured:

Increased document and information density resists discrimination by traditional search technologies. . . . Increased complexity of search tools is not likely to significantly assist the average Web searcher, whose queries include little more than two terms.

He suggests that search service providers turn their attention to developing tools to help users define an information space through which they can browse, rather than trying to help them zero in on the perfect answer. White (1996) imagined (and hoped to develop) agents that would take over the task of interacting with search engines.

I don't have to do searches *per se*, directly using these powerful indexing machines. . . . I want to use them indirectly. I want my agent to use them directly and I want to see the results, and I want to see the results in a way that's unintrusive and helpful. (p. 70)

He also refers to the need for personalized views of the Internet:

Why do we have the same experience, the same view, when we sit down at our respective browsers? . . . We have an impersonal view of that sea of information. I want a personal view that zeros me in on the one percent of the Internet that I care about. (p. 72)

Toolboxes for users, truly intelligent agents, customized personal views of the Internet, and automated digital librarians are certainly desirable. Developments on a number of research and industrial fronts look in these directions. Rudimentary agents and push services have been available for several years, and much is being learned about filtering and rule-based resource discovery. Investigations into visualization of large document spaces hold promise for offering methods of summarizing search engine results or database content. The annual Text REtrieval Conferences (TREC) have encouraged continued work on natural language processing and statistical retrieval, laying the foundations for improvements in query processing and ranking (see Chapter 6). Automated sound and image indexing (including moving images) can extend the search engine resource pool and enhance media representation (Stix, 1997). Applications of these research areas can already be seen in digital libraries and in search tools developed for intranets. However, general-content search engines have been taking small steps in the same directions.

Personalization

Services already exist that are targeted to particular users (e.g., college students or senior citizens) and in specific subject areas or information types (e.g., law or career resources). The ability to attract advertising for products directed to an identifiable market presumably defrays the costs of resource selection, evaluation, and description. At the least a restricted and selected database is less likely to render overwhelming search results. The information needs of a known user group may be easier to predict, and in some cases the data are better defined. These conditions support more parameter-rich templating in query forms and purpose-built stable classification schemes for browsing. Even general-content search engines can offer users some customization and profiling. MetaCrawler, for example, let users save and reload search preferences such as query processing, date, domain, language, results format, and media type. Many services will develop a personal "portal" for an individual, based on demographic data and identification of areas of interest. Once established, the personal page displays customized information and Web links.

Another very basic aspect of "personal service" is knowing what searching the user has just done. The ability to modify search strategies is something professional searchers take for granted in commercial online searching and is lost in the stateless world of Web searching. Many popular search engines return search results preceded by a link to a page suggesting methods for improving search results, but these help files are generic rather than specific to the particular query. In the late 1990s, several search engines introduced methods of giving the appearance of retaining search sets for modification. GO.com's Infoseek, for instance, offers a "search these results" option once hits have been returned, and commands include a pipe between query terms (e.g., "cats | food") which searches for the second term in items which contain the first. Neither of these is more than a Boolean AND (although reversing the term order in a piped statement affects ranking), and neither is at all the same as being able to manipulate sets. Still, perhaps this represents a perception that certain types of searchers need these kinds of capabilities.

Summarization

Andrews (1996) paraphrases Nick Lethaby of Verity, Inc., on the topic of search engines:

> Users don't want to interact with a search engine much beyond keying in a few words and letting it set out results. That puts the burden on the engine's vendor to make a product that gives the user the ability to find the general set of documents he or she needs without checking each document one at a time. (p. 42)

One way of doing that is to summarize results so that at least users can identify smaller sets for detailed inspection. Northern Light uses both automatic and intellectual means to classify search results into useful folders (see Figure 5.5). InFind appears to use a combination of domain names and text in the HTML <TITLE> element to organize results into categories.

Another way to reduce overload is to decrease the size of the dataset. Yahoo, GO.com's Infoseek, and Lycos, among others, offer query search restricted to specific categories in their selected and classified collections of Web pages (see Figure 5.6). Clever, under development at IBM, focuses on restricting search results to small

Figure 5.5

Northern Light Folders

Reprinted with permission of Northern Light Technology, Inc.

Figure 5.6

Search by Collection in GO.com's Infoseek

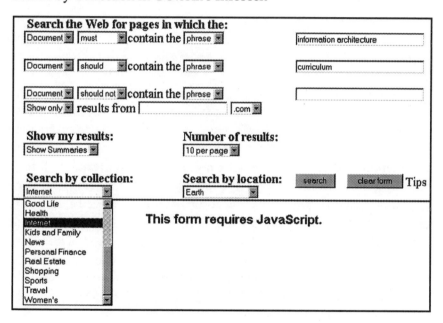

sets of the most relevant and authoritative documents using link analysis (similar to citation analysis), document text, domain, and other document characteristics (*The Clever Project*, 1998).

Query Modification

A few search engines have added query expansion or modification tools. WebZone presents additional terms culled from the retrieved set for modifying a query (see Figure 5.7), Oingo uses a lexicon to suggest query term "meanings" which may help to improve query results, and SimpliFind interacts with the user to disambiguate search terms (see Figure 5.8).

Coverage

New formats, increasing deployment of multimedia resources, and evolving markup standards cause problems for resource discovery agents (Andrews, 1997). Those search service providers that incorporate access to media do so primarily on the basis of file name extensions and text extracted from contextual materials. HotBot searches, for example, can be restricted to specific media types (image, Shockwave, JavaScript, Java, audio, Acrobat, VBScript, ActiveX, video, VRML, or a supplied extension). AltaVista's fielded search labels include "image:" and "applet:"; Lycos' specialized picture and sound retrieval utilities appear to be based on document text and file names. Advances in abstracting video, as well as research in indexing image content, should result in expanded access to multimedia files in search engines.

Subject Gateways—Different Haystacks

Another solution to the difficulty of finding the needle in the proverbial haystack is to organize the haystack. Earlier chapters in this book have looked at metadata, classification, and indexing. The advantage to search services with these types of enhancements are many—enriched representations, well-developed search and browsing tools, quality control at the selection stage, and results which

Figure 5.7

WebZone Term Suggestions

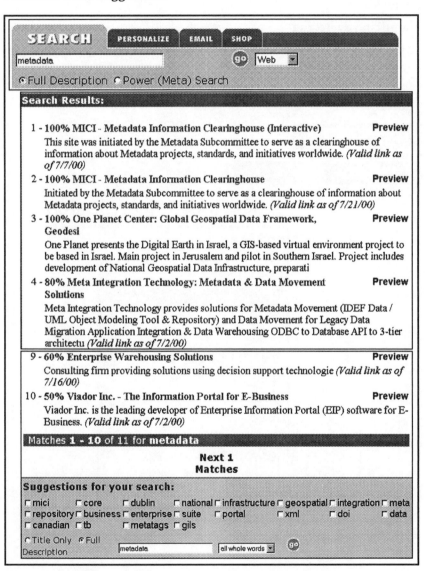

Reprinted with permission.

Figure 5.8

SimpliFind Searching

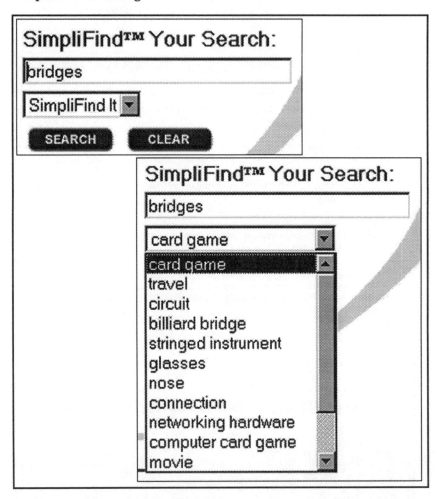

Reprinted with permission of Simpli.com, Inc., a subsidiary of NetZero, Inc., and
 Jeffrey M. Stibel.

are likely to exhibit better precision and recall. The labor costs are high, so this is not a likely model for general-content search engines. Generally, search engine agents do not retrieve content from these kinds of enhanced collections, since results are usually created on the fly from a database in response to queries. This content, along with Web-accessible OPAC records, and any other data pulled from a database and converted into HTML in response to a local search, are some examples of why the claim to index "everything on the Web" is a gross exaggeration by general-content search engines.

Smaller and better-organized subject gateways are valuable sources of selected and authoritative information. The content is, of course, specialized by region, subject, or audience, but even so it is probable that some percentage of the queries put to general search engines would be better served by these smaller, more easily navigated collections. Unfortunately, they are not in the public eye, certainly not to the degree that Yahoo, AltaVista, Excite, and others of that ilk are.

Fortunately, several directories to gateways (also called "the invisible Web") have been developed. AlphaSearch offers browsing by type or discipline through a collection of records describing full-text documents, databases, gateways, government documents, journals, news, reference tools, and search engines. Direct Search compiles "search interfaces of resources that are not easily searchable from general search tools" (Price, n.d.). InvisibleWeb.com and Webdata.com include consumer-oriented services (e.g., shopping, entertainment, and investment). Pinakes and the recently established Resource Discovery Network (RDN) provide access to well-established and respected subject gateways, many of which were developed under the United Kingdom's eLib program. Digital libraries, as they mature, will also become valuable sources of well-packaged and sometimes unique information.

Another answer to the difficulties encountered in large general search engines can be found in sites like Ask Jeeves and About.com. The former runs a query against a knowledge base of millions of "answers" and returns a list of questions with links to answers either from Ask Jeeves or from popular search engines. About.com presents a large classified collection of "expert guides" on popular topics. Then there is Webhelp, which offers live interaction with a "real live expert"—and so we end up back at the reference desk.

INTERESTING TIMES

We are at an interesting moment in information retrieval research history. It is computationally feasible to run fairly complex retrieval and ranking algorithms in large databases in a tolerable amount of real time. Existing collections of very large (if somewhat heterogeneous) databases are owned by corporations whose commercial interests are served by improvements in interface design and retrieval effectiveness. Concurrently, government and private funding initiatives support scholarly research into digital libraries, providing testbeds for exploring networked discovery and retrieval in controlled settings. Finally, there is some indication that networked information discovery will extend to both large and small collections of representations. Rarely, at least in the field of information science, do the interests of academic research and commercial product development so closely coincide. For now, the use of search engines by information professionals is often an exercise in informed frustration. There is some hope that this may change.

APPENDIX: SEARCH TIPS

General Preparation

- Read the help screens
- Look for the default settings (case sensitivity, truncation, query processing, and so on)
- Figure out the scope (the "whole" Web, selected or reviewed resources, special subjects and formats)
- Find out what experts in the field use (visit home pages)
- Figure out the indexing (full text, certain parts, stopwords)
- Break your search into concept "facets" or "blocks"
- Bookmark while you work

- Have on hand a features chart (links can be found on the Search Services Web page cited at the end of this chapter)
- Figure out the level of discovery (every site document, top-level only)

Terminology

- Come up with as much detail as you can—be "conversational"
- Use specific terminology (try to predict what might be on the page, especially in the <TITLE>)
- Use synonyms (consider Roget) and variant spellings (including American/British)
- Enter the most important word or concept first (it may affect ranking)
- More synonyms for one concept may give that concept more weight in ranking
- Avoid generic or vague terms, except in bound phrases
- Avoid common terms ("Internet," etc.)
- Search for acronyms under the acronym and the name spelled out
- Examine preliminary results for additional terminology (or use services which suggest terms)
- Check for spelling and typing errors
- Avoid homonyms

Query Features

- Use Boolean operators and nesting if available
- Use uppercase for proper nouns
- Phrases (usually in quotation marks) are helpful for precision
- Use proximity operators (if available) where word order is important

- Use truncation symbols, unless stemming is automatic
- If there is stemming, use the singular form
- If there is stemming, inhibit it when appropriate
- If there is no stemming and no truncation, enter singular and plural forms
- Look for date ranges, domain restrictions, file type limits, fielded search
- Use features which allow participation in ranking decisions

Examining Results

- If available, set a higher limit for number of hits per page
- If you don't find good stuff in the top 10 or 20, do another search or choose another engine
- Sort by site if available (although this only sorts the top x-many)
- For most purposes, choose a format which shows date and a brief summary
- Figure out whether "more like this" means "from the same site" or is really relevance feedback
- Examine "off-the-wall" hits, using the browser's Find, to see where your query terms are
- Bookmark results pages to re-execute the query
- If the hit list has multiple pages from the site, examine the one with the highest-level URL
- If you get a "file not found" error, try backing up in the URL

Finally

- Use meta-engines for a quick start
- Be persistent
- Use multiple engines routinely

- Use subject-specialized engines when appropriate
- Take notes on what worked and what did not

NOTE

This chapter is a revision of the author's 1998 publication "Web Search Engines," *Journal of the American Society for Information Science, 49*, 973–982. Reprinted by permission of John Wiley & Sons, Inc.

REFERENCES

Ackermann, Ernest, & Hartman, Karen. (1999). *The information specialist's guide to searching and researching on the Internet and the World Wide Web* (rev. ed.). Wilsonville, OR: ABF Content.

Andrews, Whit. (1996). Search engines gain tools for sifting content on the fly. *Web Week, 2*(11), 41–42.

Andrews, Whit. (1997). Searching questions. *Web Week, 3*(28), 1, 44.

Andrews, Whit. (1998). Microsoft to get $60M from engines on its hub. *Internet World, 4*(31), 1, 53.

Barry, Tony, & Richardson, Joanna. (1996, November 5). *Indexing the Net. A review of indexing tools.* Retrieved January 8, 1999 from the World Wide Web: http://www.scu.edu.au/sponsored/ausweb/ausweb96/educn/barry1/paper.html.

Bates, Mary Ellen. (1999). *Super searchers do business: The online secrets of top business researchers.* Medford, NJ: Information Today.

Berghel, Hal. (1997). Cyberspace 2000: Dealing with information overload. *Communications of the ACM, 40*(2), 19–24.

Berst, Jesse. (1998, August 17). *Search sites' shocking secret.* Retrieved January 9, 1999 from the World Wide Web: http://www.zdnet.com/anchordesk/story/story_2432.html.

Bradley, Phil. (1999). *Internet power searching: The advanced manual.* New York: Neal-Schuman.

Calliau, Robert. (1995, October 3). *A little history of the World Wide Web.* Retrieved January 8, 1999 from the World Wide Web: http://www.w3.org/History.html.

Chu, Heting, & Rosenthal, Marilyn R. (1996). Search engines for the World Wide Web: A comparative study and evaluation methodology. In Steve Hardin (Ed.), *Global complexity: Information, chaos, and control. Proceedings of the 59th ASIS Annual Meeting* (pp. 127–135).

Medford, NJ: Information Today. Also retrieved January 8, 1999 from the World Wide Web: http://www.asis.org/annual-96/ElectronicProceedings/chu.html.

Clarke, Sarah J., & Willett, Peter. (1997). Estimating the recall performance of Web search engines. *Aslib Proceedings, 49*, 184–189.

The Clever Project. (1998). Retrieved January 11, 1999 from the World Wide Web: http://www.almaden.ibm.com/cs/k53/clever.html.

Courtois, Martin P., Baer, William M., & Stark, Marcella. (1995). Cool tools for searching the Web. *Online, 19*(6), 14–32.

Ding, Wei I., & Marchionini, Gary. (1996). A comparative study of web search service performance. In S. Hardin (Ed.), *Global complexity: Information, chaos, and control: Proceedings of the 59th ASIS Annual Meeting* (pp. 136–142). Medford, NJ: Information Today.

Dong, Xiaoying, & Su, Louise T. (1997). Search engines on the World Wide Web and information retrieval from the Internet: A review and evaluation. *Online & CD-ROM Review, 21*(2), 67–81.

Feldman, Susan. (1997). Just the answers, please: Choosing a Web search service. *Searcher, 5*(5), 44–57.

Feldman, Susan. (1998). Where do we put the Web search engines? *Searcher, 6*(10), 40–46.

Gauch, Susan, & Wang, Guijun. (1996, September 8). *Information fusion with ProFusion* (Presented at WebNet '96). Retrieved January 8, 1999 from the World Wide Web: http://aace.virginia.edu/aace/conf/webnet/html/155.htm.

Gould, Cheryl. (1998). *Searching smart on the World Wide Web.* Berkeley, CA: Library Solutions Press, 1998.

Gray, Matthew. (1998, April 29). *Internet statistics: Growth and usage of the web and the Internet.* Retrieved January 8, 1999 from the World Wide Web: http://www.mit.edu/people/mkgray/net/.

Haskin, David. (1997). The right search engine: IW Labs test. *Internet World, 9.* Retrieved January 8, 1999 from the World Wide Web: http://www.iw.com/1997/09/report.html.

Hock, Randolph. (1999). *The extreme searcher's guide to Web search engines: A handbook for the serious searcher.* Medford, NJ: CyberAge Books.

Home on the Web. (1998, September 1). *PC Magazine, 17*(15). Retrieved January 8, 1999 from the World Wide Web: http://www.zdnet.com/pcmag/features/webportals/intro.html.

Jansen, Bernard J., Spink, Amanda, & Saracevic, Tefko. (2000). Real life, real users, and real needs: A study and analysis of user queries on the web. *Information Processing & Management, 36*, 207–227.

Keizer, Gregg. (1998, January 14). Search engine shootout: Top engines compared. Retrieved January 8, 1999 from the World Wide Web: http://www.cnet.com/Content/Reviews/Compare/Search2/.

Kimmel, Stacey. (1996). Robot-generated databases on the World Wide Web. *Database, 19*(1), 40–49.

Kochtanek, Thomas, Laffey, James, Ervin, Jane, Tuneder, Heather, & Borwick, Jim. (1998). Project Whistlestop: An evaluation of search engines on the Web. In M.E. Williams (Ed.), *National Online Meeting: Proceedings—1998* (pp. 211–221). Medford, NJ: Information Today.

Lake, Matthew. (1997, August 10). *2nd Annual Search Engine Shoot-out: AltaVista, Excite, HotBot, and Infoseek square off.* Retrieved January 8, 1999 from the World Wide Web: http://www4.zdnet.com/pccomp/features/excl0997/sear/sear.html.

Larsen, Ronald L. (1997, April). Relaxing assumptions, stretching the vision. *D-Lib Magazine.* Retrieved January 8, 1999 from the World Wide Web: http://www.dlib.org/april97/04larsen.html.

Lawrence, Steve, & Giles, Lee C. (1998). Searching the World Wide Web. *Science, 280*(5360), 98–100.

Leighton, H. Vernon, & Srivastava, Jaideep. (1999). First 20 precision among World Wide Web search services (search engines). *Journal of the American Society for Information Science, 50,* 870–881.

Lidsky, David & Sirapyan, Nancy. (1999, January 8). *Find it on the Web.* Retrieved January 9, 1999 from the World Wide Web: http://www.zdnet.com/products/stories/reviews/0,4161,367982,00.html

Lynch, Clifford. (1997). Searching the Internet. *Scientific American, 276*(3), 52–56.

Maze, Susan, Moxley, David, & Smith, Donna J. (1997). *Authoritative guide to Web search engines.* New York: Neal-Schuman.

Mclaughlin, Tim. (1999). Revving up the search engines. *Boston Herald,* December 27. Retrieved December 29, 1999 from the World Wide Web: http://www.businesstoday.com/techpages/srch12271999.htm.

Nahl, Diane. (1998). Ethnography of novices' first use of Web search engines: Affective control in cognitive processing. *Internet Reference Services Quarterly, 3*(2), 51–72.

Paul, Nora, & Williams, Margot. (1999). *Great scouts! Cyberguides for subject searching on the Web.* Medford, NJ: CyberAge Books.

Peterson, Richard Einer. (1997). Eight Internet search engines compared. *First Monday, 2*(2). Retrieved January 8, 1999 from the World Wide Web: http://www.firstmonday.dk/issues/issue2_2/peterson/.

Pollock, Annabel, & Hockley, Andrew. (1997, March). What's wrong with Internet searching? *D-Lib Magazine*. Retrieved January 8, 1999 from the World Wide Web: http://www.dlib.org/dlib/march97/bt/03pollock.html.

Price, Gary. (n.d.). *Direct Search*. Retrieved January 11, 1999 from the World Wide Web: http://gwis2.circ.gwu.edu/~gprice/direct.htm.

Schlichting, Carsten, & Nilsen, Erik. (1996, December 17). *Signal detection analysis of WWW search engines*. Retrieved January 8, 1999 from the World Wide Web: http://www.microsoft.com/ usability/webconf/schlichting/schlichting.htm.

Smith, Donna J., Moxley, David, & Maze, Susan. (1997). Exploiting search engines. *Business and Finance Bulletin, 105*, 17–22.

Spink, Amanda, Bateman, Judy, & Jansen, Bernard J. (1998). Users' searching behavior on the Excite Web search engine. In M.E. Williams (Ed.), *National Online Meeting: Proceedings—1998* (pp. 375–386). Medford, NJ: Information Today.

Spink, Amanda, Bateman, Judy, & Jansen, Bernard J. (1999). Searching the Web: A survey of Excite users. *Internet Research, 9*, 117–128.

Stix, Gary. (1997). Finding pictures on the Web. *Scientific American, 276*(3), 54–55.

Stobart, Simon, & Kerridge, Sue. (1996, November 8). *WWW search engine study*. Retrieved January 8, 1999 from the World Wide Web: http://osiris.sunderland.ac.uk/sst/se/.

Su, Louise T. (1997). Developing a comprehensive and systematic model of user evaluation of Web-based search engines. In M.E. Williams (Ed.), *National Online Meeting: Proceedings—1997* (pp. 335–345). Medford, NJ: Information Today.

Su, Louise T., Chen, Hsin-liang, & Dong, Xiaoying. (1998). Evaluation of Web-based search engines from the end-user's perspective: A pilot study. In C. Preston (Ed.), *Information access in the global economy: Proceedings of the 61st ASIS Annual Meeting, Pittsburgh, PA, October 24–29, 1998* (pp. 348–361). Medford, NJ: Information Today.

Tomaiuolo, Nicholas G., & Packer, Joan G. (1996). An analysis of Internet search engines: Assessment of over 200 search queries. *Computers in Libraries, 16*(6), 58–62.

Vaughan, Jason. (1999). Considerations in choice of an Internet search tool. *Library Hi Tech, 17*(1), 89–106.

Wang, Peiling, Tenopir, Carol, Layman, Elizabeth, Penniman, David, & Collins, Shawn. (1998). An exploratory study of user searching of the World Wide Web: A holistic approach. In C. Preston (Ed.), *In-*

formation access in the global economy: Proceedings of the 61st ASIS Annual Meeting, Pittsburgh, PA, October 24–29, 1998 (pp. 389–399). Medford, NJ: Information Today.

Westera, Gillian. (1997, July 4). *Robot-driven search engine evaluation: Overview.* Retrieved January 8, 1999 from the World Wide Web: http://www.curtin.edu.au/curtin/library/staffpages/gwpersonal/senginestudy/.

White, Jim. (1996). Tricks of the agent trade: General magic conjures PDA agents [Interview]. *Internet World, 7*(5), 67–76.

Xie, M., Wang, H., & Goh, T.N. (1998). Quality dimensions of Internet search engines. *Journal of Information Science, 24,* 365–372.

Zakon, Robert H. (1998, December 31). *Hobbes' Internet timeline.* Retrieved January 8, 1999 from the World Wide Web: http://info.isoc.org/guest/zakon/Internet/History/HIT.html.

Zorn, Peggy, Emanoil, Mary, Marshall, Lucy, & Panek, Mary. (1996, May). Advanced searching: Tricks of the trade. *Online, 21*(3). Retrieved January 8, 1999 from the World Wide Web: http://www.onlineinc.com/onlinemag/MayOL/zorn5.html.

WEB PAGE

Search Services. http://www.simmons.edu/~schwartz/mysearch.html.

6

Around the Corner

Is it true that "cataloging is cool" (Garman, 1999)—that we can "tame the Internet" (Lange & Winkler, 1997) or "untangle the Web" (Duda, 1996)? Perhaps we believe, with Arlene Taylor (1999), that

> the principles of organization that have developed over the
> last several hundred centuries will not be thrown out but
> will continue to evolve into the organizing principles of the
> future. (p. 228)

The question is more probably not whether we can organize the Web, but whether we can organize those parts of it which are important to our communities. This is, after all, what we have been doing in libraries for centuries. We make no pretense of trying to impose control over the entire world of knowledge, long-lasting and ephemeral. We focus on adding value to knowledge resources by evaluating and selecting them, describing them, analyzing their subject matter with standardized tools, providing pathways to them through classificatory and referencing structures, making them easy to assess with useful display formats, developing flexible interfaces, exercising quality control to ensure accuracy, and making these activities affordable through cooperative ventures.

Granted we have not perfected these arts, but their value can be seen in the projects surveyed throughout this book—projects which have involved librarians and other information professionals and which have tried to capitalize on what we have learned about subject access over the years. In fact, we should be proud of how much we have contributed and continue to contribute to developing services and mechanisms for coping with the chaos that is the Internet.

As is often the case, much of this work is unsung. Bates (1998) makes the point that, to the person outside library and information science (LIS), the information retrieval problem seems to be solved, or about to be solved, with a little tweaking of automated text retrieval techniques. She adds that researchers are underrepresented in LIS, while the field is overburdened with fundamental issues needing investigation, resulting in difficulties in developing a sustained body of research addressing these issues. We on the inside know that "effective, completely automated indexing and access to textual and text-linked databases eludes us still" (Bates, p. 1186), but that is not clear to the outsider.

As the world of digital information evolves, so do efforts to bring parts of it under control. Developments in a number of different areas bear watching for their contributions to our understanding of subject access to networked resources. Most of these fields of study are interrelated, and most are sustained by a large body of research and publication. Here they are presented briefly as an indication of branches of knowledge which have, or can be expected to have, a direct impact on approaches to organization. Where appropriate, directions are given for further reading and exploration.

MACHINE-AIDED INDEXING

Even when assignment of subject headings and classification numbers is largely an intellectual process, indexers rely on assistance from computer processing. This might take the form of online thesauri and number-building tools, lookups to past practice (e.g., how has this index term been used in this file so far), error checking and validation, or simply general clerical support. Machine Aided Indexing (MAI) routines go a step further by attempting to perform indexing or classification. This is especially useful, if not essential, in settings with a high volume of new documents and the need for speedy throughput.

MAI can be used to augment or extend the results of human indexing, or to recommend indexing based on automatic examination of text (see Figure 6.1). In Hodge and Milstead's (1998) review of computer support for indexing, the following types of MAI processes can be discerned:

- Working with the results of indexer assignment (1) to derive authorized terms or (2) to validate assigned terms.

- Working with document text (full text, or more commonly titles and abstracts) (1) to identify specific types of terms (e.g., proper names) or (2) to suggest indexing terms from a thesaurus, either by using a rule base or by using automated text processing algorithms.

In many cases, MAI routines incorporate learning, both from past practice in an existing database and from human assessment of MAI results. In presenting the MAI product marketed by Access Innovations, Ven Eman (1999) suggests that MAI can improve indexer consistency, produce "deeper" indexing, and significantly increase indexer productivity. MAI applications are largely developed for specific settings (e.g., LEXIS-NEXIS' SmartIndexing Technology), but several companies market MAI software (the best known is Access Innovations), and related research comes out of the field of text mining (see below).

AUTOMATED TEXT PROCESSING

As mentioned in Chapter 4, research into automated text processing has a long and distinguished history, going back to the 1950s and the beginning of computer processing of machine-readable text. Initially based primarily on counting words and calculating word co-occurrences, techniques for retrieval from text have progressed

Figure 6.1

Data Harmony's Machine-Aided Indexer

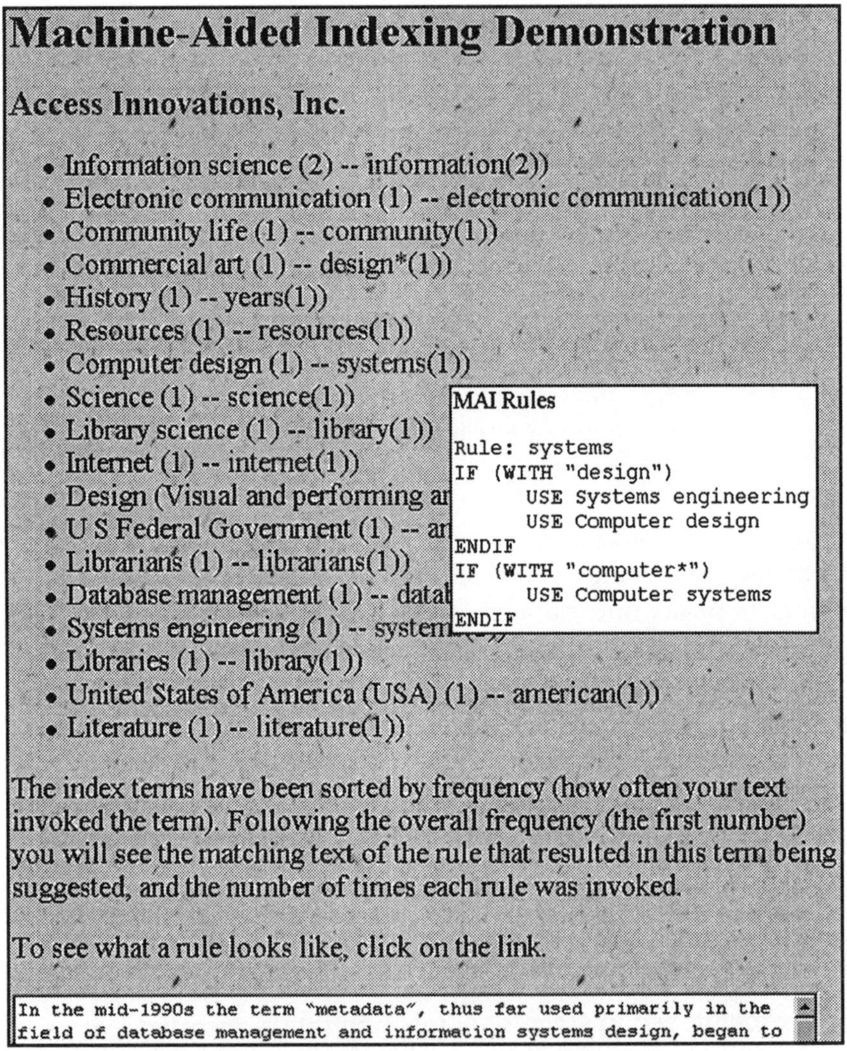

Machine-Aided Indexing Demonstration

Access Innovations, Inc.

- Information science (2) -- information(2))
- Electronic communication (1) -- electronic communication(1))
- Community life (1) -- community(1))
- Commercial art (1) -- design*(1))
- History (1) -- years(1))
- Resources (1) -- resources(1))
- Computer design (1) -- systems(1))
- Science (1) -- science(1))
- Library science (1) -- library(1))
- Internet (1) -- internet(1))
- Design (Visual and performing ar
- U S Federal Government (1) -- an
- Librarians (1) -- librarians(1))
- Database management (1) -- datab
- Systems engineering (1) -- system
- Libraries (1) -- library(1))
- United States of America (USA) (1) -- american(1))
- Literature (1) -- literature(1))

```
MAI Rules

Rule: systems
IF (WITH "design")
     USE Systems engineering
     USE Computer design
ENDIF
IF (WITH "computer*")
     USE Computer systems
ENDIF
```

The index terms have been sorted by frequency (how often your text invoked the term). Following the overall frequency (the first number) you will see the matching text of the rule that resulted in this term being suggested, and the number of times each rule was invoked.

To see what a rule looks like, click on the link.

```
In the mid-1990s the term "metadata", thus far used primarily in the
field of database management and information systems design, began to
```

Reprinted with permission. Data Harmony is the product company of Access Innovations, Inc.

to include many different kinds of statistical or probabilistic procedures, and to incorporate methods from cognitive sciences, linguistics, and other allied disciplines. Some more common applications include:

- Information retrieval and ranking of results;
- Relevance feedback ("I like this item, find me more like it," or "I don't like this item, remove others like it from my results");
- Document clustering and automatic classification (e.g., of retrieved results or information spaces); and
- Term clustering (e.g., for query modification or concept structure building).

Although each has a slightly different emphasis, either of the recent textbooks by Korfhage (1997) and Meadow, Boyce, and Kraft (2000) is a good source for reviewing the fundamentals of text-based information retrieval. Feldman's (1999) succinct overview of natural language processing (NLP) is a fine general introduction to this specific area, and can be followed by Liddy's (1998) discussion of NLP in information retrieval (IR) and Haas' (1996) state-of-the-art review. Current research is found in the journals *Information Processing & Management*, *Information Retrieval*, and the *Journal of the American Society for Information Science*, and in the proceedings of the annual International ACM SIGIR Conference on Research and Development in Information Retrieval.

Recently, the annual Text REtrieval Conference (TREC), co-sponsored by the U.S. National Institute of Standards and Technology (NIST) and the U.S. Defense Advanced Research Projects Agency (DARPA), has had a significant impact on progress and communication in this field by providing collection testbeds against which information retrieval researchers can test performance effectiveness. Involvement in TREC has expanded to the point where, in its seventh year, participants represented 56 groups, including 13 countries and over 20 companies (*Text REtrieval Conference [TREC] Overview*, 1999).

Text Mining

Text mining is a recent extrapolation of data mining, more generally called knowledge discovery in databases (KDD). Data mining uses computer-driven algorithms and modeling to analyze large collections of data in support of business decision making. In combination with huge warehouses of reasonably well-structured data (primarily internally generated), data mining allows a company to make the most of its knowledge by revealing patterns, relationships, and predictive models that would otherwise be difficult to discern. Text mining takes the ideas of data mining and carries them forward to the environment of large bodies of poorly structured data, that is, text databases, including collections of Web documents.

KDD techniques include:

- Classification to predetermined categories, like MAI;
- Clustering based on some measure of similarity;
- Association (illuminating interrelationships among data);
- Sequencing (revealing inherent order in the data); and
- Link analysis (analyzing link-to patterns of items).

Many companies sell data mining software, either as separate products or as part of knowledge management suites. Text mining applications are not quite so common, but a few examples of more well-known products can illustrate the diversity of solutions to the text knowledge management problem:

- Dataware uses the INQUERY search engine and other tools to retrieve and analyze information across large distributed collections of items in diverse formats;
- Semio focuses on interactive graphical representations of the results of automatic clustering; and
- TextWise uses sophisticated statistical and natural language processing to perform retrieval, information extraction, visualization, knowledge discovery, and cross-language searching.

Zorn, Emanoil, Marshall, and Panek's (1999) brief introduction to text mining is a very useful overview. Trybula's (1997) state-of-the-art review of data mining and knowledge discovery is an excellent source for a deeper look. Two recent journal issues explore issues, applications, and trends—the *Journal of the American Society for Information Science* (Raghavan, Deogun, & Sever, 1998) looks at a number of different KDD methods, and *Library Trends* (Qin & Norton, 1999) examines KDD in bibliographic databases.

Whether achieved through KDD or MAI, the advantages of automating some part of the subject representation process cannot be denied:

> Using models such as classification and clustering against the raw data contained on the Web can automate the indexing process, creating custom indexing and categorization based on criteria specified either by the mining model or even the searcher or end-user. Automating the indexing process can overcome the problems of ownership and sheer size presented by the Web, and the intelligence of mining tools makes it possible to better handle the wealth of unstructured data available on the Internet and intranets. (Zorn, Emanoil, Marshall, & Panek, 1999, p. 20)

Visualization

Visualization, long an area of study in science, is becoming more popular as an element of information retrieval and knowledge discovery interfaces. Automated text retrieval in general, and KDD applications in particular, benefit from presenting information spaces or resources visually. As one obvious example, the bigger an information result (from the retrieval point of view, the broader the query or the higher the recall), the more difficult it is to sift through linear lists to find relevant items. Visual information retrieval interfaces (VIRI) such as VR-VIBE and LyberWorld (two of the earliest) combine automated text processing and graphical modelling to map items into information spaces. Xia Lin's Sitemap plots documents into an information space, using extracted terms to create labels for clustered items. Figure 6.2 shows a Sitemap for the Yahoo category Space Science. TileBars, developed by Marti Hearst, renders a visual representation of the frequency and co-occurrence of sets of query terms in long text documents (see Figure 6.3). The UC Berkeley Digital Library uses an adaptation of TileBars for access to a collection of California environmental information.

Most visualization projects are still in research and development, but Web directories such as McKiernan's *The Big Picture(sm)* (http://www.public.iastate.edu/~CYBERSTACKS/BigPic.htm) and TeleGeography's *Atlas of Cyberspaces* (http://www.cybergeography. com/atlas/atlas.html), especially the Info Maps and Info Spaces sections, bear witness to the growth of interest in this field. Williams, Sochats, and Morse's (1995) state-of-the-art review, while dated, is a good source for basic concepts and an historical overview. White and McCain (1997), although writing specifically about visualization of literatures, also bring general IR visualization up to date. Applications presented in a recent collection edited by Rorvig (1999) include science maps based on citation data, interactive graphical interfaces for bibliographic databases, and visual thesauri. Visualization is definitely a space worth watching.

FINAL THOUGHTS

This book has taken subject access to collections of Web-accessible networked resources as its focus, and especially the use of "traditional" subject analysis tools. This final chapter briefly surveys related research based largely on automatic tools and techniques. A theme running through the entire text is the likelihood of increasing collaboration between the traditional and the automatic, capitalizing on the strengths of both. Such collaboration will be fortified by application areas where software engineers meet librarians—two examples which come to mind are digital libraries (DLs) and knowledge management (KM).

Many digital libraries use thesauri and classification schemes as access systems, and as DLs grow in size they will be useful testbeds for subject access study. Furthermore, digital library research is concerned not only with resource discovery within the confines of one

Figure 6.2

Sitemap

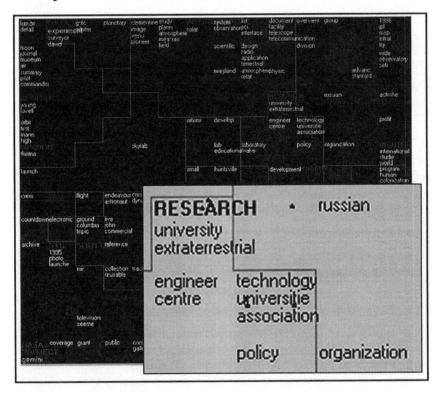

Reprinted with permission.

Figure 6.3

TileBars

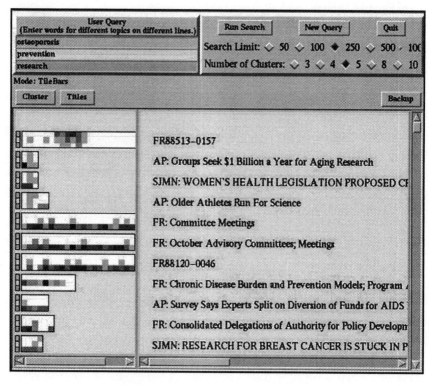

Reprinted with permission.

(usually distributed) DL, but also with interoperability of discovery tools between DLs (e.g., see Buckland, 1999; Kirremuir et al., 1998).

Knowledge management is concerned with leveraging the formal and informal knowledge of an organization so that employees can make well-informed business decisions and increase productivity, and so that the organization can gain a competitive advantage. Knowledge resources, which can include everything from individuals to e-mail to formal publications, need to be organized and described for effective access, and although resource organization is just one aspect of knowledge management, it is the point where LIS has much to contribute ("new opportunities," as Marshall [1997] puts it).

For their millennium issue, the editors of the journal *Searcher* asked a number of experts to peer into the future. Feldman (2000) posits the ideal information retrieval scenario ("the answer machine") and looks at how far we have come and how far we have to go. Her future includes a combination of new technologies, NLP tools, and the expertise of information professionals in access systems design. In the same issue, in a list of hypothetical (and both amusing and terrifying) news briefs from the future, Clifford Lynch (2000) includes the following:

> By 2010, a number of technologies—filtering, personal agents, recommender systems, sophisticated information merging and summarization and correlation, and effective selective dissemination of information—have been coupled to the personal information appliance and have brought the sense of information overload under control. (p. 87)

Ten years is a long way away in Internet time, and it worth noting the use of the phrase "*sense* of information control," perhaps implying perception rather than reality.

Nonetheless, it is not too much of a stretch to believe that by the end of another decade much of what is currently human-driven subject analysis will be done by machine. In fact, given the growth in digital information and the comparative paucity of catalogers and indexers, many aspects of subject-based resource description and discovery will have to be automated. However, these emerging and as-yet-undiscovered automatic methods will owe some of their success to what we have learned, and are still learning, from studying intellectual subject analysis—its processes, applications, and implications for retrieval systems and users.

REFERENCES

Bates, Marcia J. (1998). Indexing and access for digital libraries and the Internet: Human, database, and domain factors. *Journal of the American Society for Information Science, 49*, 1185–1205.

Buckland, Michael. (1999). Mapping entry vocabulary to unfamiliar metadata vocabularies. *D-Lib Magazine, 5*(1). Retrieved August 30, 2000 from the World Wide Web: http://www.dlib.org/dlib/january99/buckland/01buckland.html.

Duda, Andrea L. (Ed.). (1996). *Untangling the Web: proceedings of the conference sponsored by the Librarians Association of the University of California, Santa Barbara and Friends of the UCSB Library, April 26, 1996.* Retrieved December 31, 1999 from the World Wide Web: http://www.library.ucsb.edu/untangle/.

Feldman, Susan. (1999). NLP meets the jabberwocky: Natural language processing in information retrieval. *Online, 23*(3), 62–72.

Feldman, Susan. (2000). The answer machine. *Searcher, 8*(1), 58–78.

Garman, Nancy. (1999). Now that cataloging is cool. *Online, 23*(5), 6.

Haas, Stephanie W. (1996). Natural language processing: Toward large-scale, robust systems. *Annual Review of Information Science and Technology, 31*, 83–119.

Hodge, Gail M., & Milstead, Jessica L. (1998). *Computer support to indexing.* Philadelphia: National Federation of Abstracting and Information Services.

Kirremuir, John, Brickley, Dan, Welsh, Susan, Knight, Jon, & Hamilton, Martin. (1998, January). Cross-searching subject gateways. *D-Lib Magazine, 4*(1). Retrieved January 4, 2000 from the World Wide Web: http://www.dlib.org/dlib/january98/01kirriemuir.html.

Korfhage, Robert R. (1997). *Information storage and retrieval.* New York: Wiley.

Lange, Holley R., & Winkler, B. Jean. (1997). Taming the Internet: Metadata, a work in progress. *Advances in Librarianship, 21*, 47–72.

Liddy, Elizabeth D. (1998). Enhanced text retrieval using natural language processing. *Bulletin of the American Society for Information Science*, 24(4), 14–16.

Lynch, Clifford. (2000). Notes and fragments. *Searcher*, 8(1), 86–89.

Marshall, Lucy. (1997). Facilitating knowledge management and knowledge sharing: New opportunities for information professionals. *Online*, 21(5), 92–98.

Meadow, Charles T., Boyce, Bert R., & Kraft, Donald H. (2000). *Text information retrieval systems*. San Diego, CA: Academic Press.

Qin, Jian, & Norton, M. Jay. (Eds.). (1999). Knowledge discovery in bibliographic databases. *Library Trends*, 48(1).

Raghavan, Vijay V., Deogun, Jitender S., & Sever, Hayri (Eds.). (1998). Special topic issue: Knowledge discovery and data mining. *Journal of the American Society for Information Science*, 49(5).

Rorvig, Mark E. (Ed.). (1999). Perspectives on visual information retrieval interfaces. *Journal of the American Society for Information Science*, 50 (9).

Taylor, Arlene G. (1999). *The organization of information*. Englewood, CO: Libraries Unlimited.

Text REtrieval Conference (TREC) Overview. (1999, February 23). Retrieved December 31, 1999 from the World Wide Web: http://trec.nist.gov/overview.html.

Trybula, Walter J. (1997). Data mining and knowledge discovery. *Annual Review of Information Science and Technology*, 32, 197–229.

Ven Eman, Jay. (1999, June 24). *Intranet access to your organisation's knowledge: Promises and challenges*. Retrieved January 3, 2000 from the World Wide Web: http://www.accessinn.com/agsi/index.htm.

White, Howard D., & McCain, Katherine W. (1997). Visualization of literatures. *Annual Review of Information Science and Technology*, 32, 99–167.

Williams, James G., Sochats, Kenneth M., & Morse, Emile. (1995). Visualization. *Annual Review of Information Science and Technology*, 30, 161–207.

Zorn, Peggy, Emanoil, Mary, Marshall, Lucy, & Panek, Mary. (1999). Finding needles in the haystack: Mining meets the Web. *Online*, 23(5), 17–28.

Author Index

Subject Index

About the Author

CANDY SCHWARTZ is a professor in the Graduate School of Library and Information Science at Simmons College. Her teaching activities focus on information organization and retrieval, including subject analysis, database management, records management, Web site development, and digital libraries. She has recently served as President of the American Society for Information Science and Technology and is co-editor of *Library and Information Science Research*, a quarterly refereed journal focusing on research methodologies and applications. She is co-author of *Records Management and the Library* (Ablex, 1993), and her recent publications have appeared in the *Journal of the American Society for Information Science* and the *Journal of Academic Librarianship*.